OPPOSITIONAL DEFIANT DISORDER SIMPLIFIED:

PRACTICAL PARENTING TIPS FOR EFFECTIVE COMMUNICATION, EMOTIONAL SUPPORT, AND BEHAVIOR MANAGEMENT TO IMPROVE YOUR FAMILY DYNAMIC

CHARLENE COLLINS

CONTENTS

Introduction 7

1. UNDERSTANDING ODD AND ITS FOUNDATIONS 11
   1.1 Decoding ODD: Symptoms and Diagnosis
Criteria 11
   1.2 The Psychological Landscape of ODD: What
Happens in the Brain? 14
   1.3 How ODD Differs from Other Behavioral
Disorders 16
   1.4 Setting the Stage: Early Signs and Intervention
Strategies 18

2. EFFECTIVE COMMUNICATION STRATEGIES 21
   2.1 Active Listening Skills for Tough Conversations 21
   2.2 The Role of Body Language in Communicating
with Your Child 23
   2.3 Conflict Resolution Techniques That
Really Work 26
   2.4 Using Validation to Build Empathy 28
   2.5 Age-Appropriate Communication Tactics 30

3. PRACTICAL BEHAVIOR MANAGEMENT
TECHNIQUES 33
   3.1 Positive Reinforcement and Reward Systems 34
   3.2 Establishing and Maintaining Consistent
Routines 37
   3.3 Consequences vs. Punishment: A Balanced
Approach 39
   3.4 De-escalating Techniques During Outbursts 41

4. HANDLING EVERYDAY CHALLENGES 45
   4.1 Morning Routines Without the Battle 45
   4.2 Managing Public Outbursts 48
   4.3 Dealing with School-Related Issues 50
   4.4 Handling Disrespect and Aggression at Home 53
   4.5 Strategies for Bedtime Resistance 55

5. BUILDING POSITIVE FAMILY RELATIONSHIPS   59

    5.1 Daily Practices to Strengthen Parent-Child Connections   59

    5.2 Positive Reinforcement Techniques That Actually Work   62

    5.3 The Role of Quality Time in Building Trust   64

    5.4 Addressing Parental Needs and Relationship Strains   66

    5.5 Celebrating Small Wins with Your Family   68

6. HOLISTIC AND ALTERNATIVE APPROACHES   75

    6.1 Diet, Nutrition, and ODD: What Parents Should Know   76

    6.2 The Role of Exercise in Managing ODD   79

    6.3 Mindfulness Practices for Kids and Parents   81

    6.4 The Impact of Art and Music Therapy   84

    6.5 Homeopathy and Herbal Supplements: What Parents Should Know   87

7. THERAPEUTIC INTERVENTIONS AND SUPPORTS   91

    7.1 Cognitive Behavioral Therapy: A Guide for Parents   91

    7.2 Understanding the Role of Medication   95

    7.3 The Importance of School-Based Interventions   98

    7.4 Navigating Insurance and Access to Therapies   101

    7.5 How Support Groups Can Help Your Family   103

8. PARENTAL SELF-CARE AND STRESS MANAGEMENT   107

    8.1 Simple Self-Care Practices for Busy Parents   108

    8.2 Stress Management Techniques That Promote Wellbeing   110

    8.3 Building a Support Network: Finding Community   112

    8.4 Balancing Parenting and Personal Life   115

9. EMPOWERMENT THROUGH UNDERSTANDING AND ACTION   119

    9.1 Advocating for Your Child in Various Settings   120

    9.2 The Importance of Consistent Parenting Techniques   123

    9.3 Educating Relatives and Friends About ODD   125

9.4 The Future of ODD: Trends and Research   128

9.5 When to Update Your Strategies: Signs of
Evolving Needs   131

9.6 Harnessing Technology: Apps and Tools for
Managing ODD   134

10. REAL-LIFE SUCCESS STORIES AND CASE
STUDIES   137

10.1 Overcoming Severe Defiance: A Family's
Journey   137

10.2 Innovative School Approaches That Worked   139

10.3 Therapy Breakthroughs: Children's
Testimonials   141

10.4 Parents' Strategies That Turned Behavior
Around   143

Conclusion   147

References   151

INTRODUCTION

As the sun rises, you find yourself bracing for the morning routine. Getting your child ready for school transforms into a battleground over every small task—from brushing teeth to putting on shoes. Each request you make is met with defiance, and each guideline is challenged. Amid these daily struggles, a sense of isolation creeps in; it feels like no one truly understands your life's emotional rollercoaster. If you're nodding along, feeling the weight of these words, you're not alone. This is a glimpse into the world of parenting a child with Oppositional Defiant Disorder (ODD).

This book is born out of a profound desire to bridge the gap between the challenges you face and the peaceful family dynamics you aspire to create. My journey into the complexities of ODD began with personal encounters, leading to an unwavering commitment to support families like yours. Through this book, I aim to demystify ODD and provide you with practical tools and strategies that you can implement immediately to enhance communication, manage behavior effectively, and nurture a supportive family environment.

Here, you will find a blend of proven techniques and innovative approaches that address the symptoms and the underlying emotional needs that often go unspoken. From understanding the foundations of ODD in our first chapter through exploring effective communication techniques and behavioral management strategies to embracing holistic approaches and ensuring your own well-being, this book offers a comprehensive guide to transforming your familial relationships.

Consider these statistics: Approximately 1 in 10 children are diagnosed with ODD in various degrees of severity. This disorder impacts the child's life at home and school and significantly affects their social interactions and personal development. The urgency to address these issues cannot be overstated, as the long-term implications can extend into adulthood, affecting individual and professional relationships.

Yet, despite these challenges, there is hope. This book is not merely about managing a disorder, but about thriving as a family. It's about turning daily struggles into opportunities for growth and deeper connection. I invite you to approach this resource with an open mind and heart, ready to explore the practical and heartfelt advice drawn from real-life successes and evidence-based practices.

Each chapter is structured to be engaging and actionable. I encourage you to participate in this journey actively: make notes, highlight what resonates, and apply the exercises and strategies discussed. This book is designed to be a dynamic tool that grows with you and your family.

Let's begin this journey with the promise that understanding, improvement, and empowerment are possible and within reach. Let this book be your companion as you navigate the challenges of ODD, transforming them into stepping stones for a more harmonious and fulfilling family life.

CHAPTER 1

UNDERSTANDING ODD AND ITS FOUNDATIONS

Every day, parents around the globe face unique challenges that test their patience, resilience, and parenting skills. Yet, for those dealing with Oppositional Defiant Disorder (ODD), these challenges can be particularly intense. Maybe today was one of those days when everything felt like a battle, from getting your child dressed to handling their homework. It's not just the frequency of these battles that wears you down; it's their intensity and the emotional drain accompanying each episode. This chapter aims to equip you with a deeper understanding of ODD, shedding light on the symptoms, diagnosis criteria, and your critical role in effectively managing this disorder.

1.1 DECODING ODD: SYMPTOMS AND DIAGNOSIS CRITERIA

Oppositional Defiant Disorder manifests in a variety of behaviors that extend beyond the occasional tantrum or argumentative episode typical in childhood development. Children with ODD exhibit a pattern of angry, irritable mood, argumentative/defiant behavior, or vindictiveness lasting at least six months. Unlike the occasional bouts of stubbornness seen in most children, those with ODD may seem perpetually resistant to authority and frequently engage in behavior that deliberately annoys others, refuses to comply with requests, and argues excessively with adults. These behaviors are more intense and occur more frequently than is typically observed in individuals of a similar developmental level.

Diagnosing ODD involves more than identifying frequent temper tantrums or defiance. According to the Diagnostic and Statistical Manual of Mental Disorders, Fifth Edition (DSM-5), several criteria must be met for diagnosing ODD. These include at least four symptoms from categories such as angry and irritable mood, argumentative and defiant behavior, or vindictiveness, occurring most often with individuals the child knows well. These behaviors must cause significant impairment in social, educational, or occupational functioning, and they must not occur exclusively during another mental disorder. For parents and caregivers, understanding these criteria is crucial, not only for recognizing the disorder but also for seeking appropriate intervention. It's important to note that these behaviors are consistent and recurrent; a bad week at school doesn't necessarily mean a child has ODD.

As a parent, your observations are invaluable in the diagnostic process. Detailed notes on your child's behavior, the frequency, the context in which these behaviors occur, and how they differ from their peers can provide essential insights for healthcare providers. These notes can be critical in distinguishing between regular behavioral boundaries testing, which is a part of growing up, and the more persistent patterns seen in ODD.

Early diagnosis and intervention can significantly alter the trajectory of ODD. By identifying and addressing the disorder early, you can help mitigate its effects on your child's education, social interactions, and overall quality of life. For instance, early therapeutic intervention might involve teaching your child healthier ways to respond to authority or frustration, potentially curbing the escalation of the disorder into more severe conditions like conduct disorder or more entrenched behavioral patterns in adulthood.

Case Study

Consider the case of eight-year-old Marcus, who was frequently reprimanded at school for talking back to teachers and starting conflicts with peers. His parents noticed similar behaviors at home and initially attributed them to Marcus asserting his independence. However, as his behavior grew more consistent and began affecting his school work and friendships, they consulted a psychologist. With detailed notes and specific examples from both school and home, they were able to quickly get a diagnosis. Early intervention, including behavior therapy and parent training, helped Marcus learn more productive ways to express his feelings and deal with conflict, leading to noticeable improvements at school and home.

This understanding of ODD provides a foundation for managing the disorder. It empowers you as a parent to take proactive steps in supporting your child's development and well-being. As we explore further into the strategies and interventions that can be applied, remember that your knowledge and involvement are pivotal in navigating the challenges of ODD.

1.2 THE PSYCHOLOGICAL LANDSCAPE OF ODD: WHAT HAPPENS IN THE BRAIN?

Understanding the brain's functioning in children with Oppositional Defiant Disorder (ODD) offers invaluable insights into why these children may react or behave differently from their peers. Research in neurology and psychology suggests that some regions of the brain, like the frontal cortex and the amygdala, play crucial roles in emotion regulation and behavior control, which are often areas of difficulty for those with ODD. The frontal cortex, responsible for decision-making, problem-solving, and controlling impulses, may not coordinate as expected with the amygdala, the part of the brain that processes emotions. Picture the brain as a complex control room where the frontal cortex is supposed to manage emotional responses triggered by the amygdala. In children with ODD, it's as though the manager (the frontal cortex) isn't communicating effectively with the emotion center (the amygdala), leading to less control over impulses and more frequent emotional outbursts.

This miscommunication can manifest as the challenging behaviors typical of ODD—quick temper flares, defiance, and irritability. Understanding this link between brain function and behavior can significantly shift how we respond to and support children with ODD. Rather than viewing their behaviors strictly as disciplinary issues, recognizing them as part of a neurological condition can encourage a more empathetic and supportive approach. It suggests that these children aren't just acting out willfully but are struggling with managing their emotional and behavioral impulses due to their brain's unique wiring.

Moreover, the concept of neuroplasticity brings a hopeful dimension to treating ODD. Neuroplasticity refers to the brain's ability to change and adapt over time, which means the right interventions can literally reshape the brain's functioning, improving the coordination between the frontal cortex and the amygdala. Effective interventions include behavioral therapies that focus on developing emotional regulation and impulse control skills, potentially strengthening the neural pathways that facilitate better coordination between these brain regions.

Recent studies underscore the potential of such interventions. For instance, cognitive-behavioral therapy (CBT), a treatment that encourages changes in thought and behavior patterns, has been shown to promote changes in brain function associated with improved regulation of emotions and behaviors. One study published in the "Journal of Child Psychology and Psychiatry" demonstrated that children with behavioral disorders, including ODD, who underwent CBT showed significant improvements in their behavior and brain activity patterns related to emotional control and aggression management.

These findings are not just clinically significant; they offer a message of hope to parents and educators—that there is a real possibility for positive change with the proper support and interventions. The brain's adaptability means the current challenges can evolve into improved behavior and emotional responses, transforming daily interactions and overall quality of life. This understanding should empower parents with a renewed perspective on managing ODD, emphasizing the importance of targeted interventions supporting brain development and behavioral change. Through such informed approaches, we can better meet the needs of children with ODD, guiding them toward more successful and fulfilling interactions and behaviors.

1.3 HOW ODD DIFFERS FROM OTHER BEHAVIORAL DISORDERS

Navigating the landscape of behavioral disorders can often feel like trying to find your way through a maze without a map, especially when it comes to distinguishing between disorders that share several overlapping symptoms, such as Oppositional Defiant Disorder (ODD) and Attention Deficit Hyperactivity Disorder (ADHD), or differentiating ODD from Conduct Disorder (CD). Understanding these distinctions is crucial not only for accurate diagnosis, but also for effective management and treatment. Let's delve into these differences with practical guidance and real-life scenarios illuminating the path more clearly.

Firstly, comparing ODD and ADHD, two disorders are often mentioned in the same breath due to their common characteristics, such as impulsivity and challenges with authority. Both disorders manifest in early childhood and can significantly impact a child's social interactions and academic performance. However, the core of ADHD lies in inattention, hyperactivity, and impulsivity, which are not primarily driven by the mood or attitude toward authority that characterizes ODD. A child with ADHD might interrupt in class, fidget incessantly, or fail to complete tasks, not out of defiance but due to difficulty controlling impulses and maintaining focus.

In contrast, ODD primarily involves an ongoing pattern of angry or irritable mood, defiant behavior, and vindictiveness. For instance, while both children with ADHD and ODD might refuse to follow instructions, the child with ODD might do so in a confrontational manner, arguing back or deliberately annoying others. In contrast, a child with ADHD might simply be distracted and not follow through. Understanding these nuances is vital. For example, consider Michael, a 10-year-old diagnosed with ODD, who often flatly refuses to do his homework, stating it's stupid and no one can force him to do it. This contrasts with Jenny, who has ADHD and frequently forgets her assignments or gets so distracted by other stimuli that she doesn't complete them.

Moving on to differentiating ODD from Conduct Disorder (CD), this distinction is particularly critical as CD involves more severe behavioral issues. Conduct Disorder is characterized by behaviors that violate societal norms and the rights of others, such as aggression towards people and animals, destruction of property, and severe violations of rules. While ODD might involve arguing with adults or defying rules, it doesn't include the aggressive or destructive behaviors seen in CD. For instance, while a child with ODD might argue vehemently against curfew, a child with CD might respond by sneaking out, vandalizing property, or even engaging in physical altercations.

Comorbidity, or the presence of more than one disorder in a person, further complicates the landscape. It's not uncommon for a child with ODD to also experience disorders such as anxiety or depression. This overlap can affect the management and treatment strategies significantly. For example, Sarah, diagnosed with both ODD and anxiety, might exhibit defiance and irritability that are partly fueled by her anxiety about perceived expectations or social interactions. In such cases, treatment must address both the anxiety and the behavioral responses to effectively manage her overall condition.

Understanding these distinctions and overlaps not only aids in accurate diagnosis but also informs more tailored and effective intervention strategies. Each child's situation is unique, and recognizing the particular nuances of their behavioral challenges is the first step in providing the support that can lead to meaningful improvements in their lives and the family dynamic. Whether it's navigating school settings, family relationships, or social interactions, the insights gained from clear differentiation can guide more effective management approaches, fostering environments that encourage positive development despite the challenges these disorders might pose.

1.4 SETTING THE STAGE: EARLY SIGNS AND INTERVENTION STRATEGIES

Recognizing the early signs of Oppositional Defiant Disorder (ODD) in young children can often be likened to understanding the early warning signals of a brewing storm. In the case of ODD, these signs may manifest as persistent stubbornness and frequent, intense temper tantrums that stand out due to their severity compared to typical childhood behaviors. For instance, while many children might resist bedtime occasionally, a child showing early signs of ODD might consistently refuse to comply with bedtime or other routine activities, reacting with disproportionate anger or defiance. These behaviors are not just the typical trials of parenting; they're persistent and pervasive enough to disrupt daily routines and stand out as excessive.

Beyond individual behavior, the environment surrounding a child plays a pivotal role in either exacerbating or mitigating the development of ODD. Parenting styles that are either overly rigid or excessively permissive can contribute to the manifestation of defiance and oppositional behaviors in children. Similarly, family dynamics marked by high conflict, inconsistency in rules, and lack of clear communication can create an atmosphere that may foster or further aggravate the symptoms of ODD. On the other hand, supportive, nurturing, and structured environments can do much to temper potential symptoms.

School environments also significantly impact children with or at risk for ODD. In classrooms where teachers provide clear expectations and consistent consequences, children learn to understand the boundaries of acceptable behavior. Conversely, in environments that lack these structures or where punitive measures are the norm rather than supportive interventions, children may respond by increasing oppositional behaviors, which can confirm and even harden the path toward more severe manifestations of ODD.

Given these nuances, early intervention becomes a key strategy in altering the trajectory of a child showing signs of ODD. One of the most effective approaches is the implementation of consistent parenting techniques. This doesn't just mean enforcing rules consistently, though that's undoubtedly important. It also involves consistent communication and emotional engagement with the child, helping them understand that the boundaries set are out of care and concern for their well-being. For example, using clear and calm communication to explain why certain behaviors are unacceptable helps the child understand the rationale behind the rules rather than seeing them as arbitrary.

Positive reinforcement is another crucial strategy. This involves acknowledging and rewarding positive behaviors more than punishing undesirable ones. When a child with ODD experiences recognition for positive actions, such as sharing toys or following instructions, it reinforces their ability to associate these positive behaviors with positive outcomes. This reinforcement encourages more frequent occurrences of the desired behavior. Structured routines also play a critical role in managing ODD. Routines provide a predictable environment that can reduce anxiety and oppositional behaviors. Children with ODD often respond well to clear schedules that allow them to know what is expected and when which reduces uncertainty and the behavioral issues that can stem from it.

These strategies, woven into the fabric of daily interactions, are not just about managing symptoms, but about fundamentally improving the child's and family's quality of life. By setting a consistent and supportive stage early on, we can guide children toward more adaptive behaviors and provide them with the tools they need to succeed in managing their emotions and reactions, which are invaluable skills that will serve them well beyond childhood.

CHAPTER 2
EFFECTIVE COMMUNICATION STRATEGIES

Communication is the cornerstone of human connection, and its importance is magnified when parenting a child with Oppositional Defiant Disorder (ODD). It's like attempting to complete a puzzle when the pieces are constantly moving, reflecting ODD's dynamic and often unpredictable nature. With each day presenting its unique set of challenges, techniques that were effective yesterday may not hold the same impact today. This chapter is designed to provide you with a variety of effective communication strategies specifically tailored to navigate these shifting dynamics, thereby enhancing understanding and cooperation between you and your child.

2.1 ACTIVE LISTENING SKILLS FOR TOUGH CONVERSATIONS

Effective communication with your child, especially in challenging situations, begins with a fundamental skill often overlooked in the heat of the moment: active listening. Active listening involves fully concentrating on what is being said rather than passively hearing the speaker's message. It is about listening to understand, not just to respond. This approach is crucial when dealing with children who have ODD, as it can significantly de-escalate potential conflicts.

Reflective listening is a core component of active listening. It involves mirroring back what your child has said, demonstrating that you understand their feelings and thoughts. This doesn't mean you have to agree with them, but it does mean acknowledging their feelings as valid. For instance, if your child says, "You never listen to me!" instead of immediately getting defensive, you could reflect by saying, "It sounds like you're feeling ignored, and that's hard for you." This indicates that you are paying attention to their feelings and trying to understand their perspective, which can help soothe frustrations and open the door to more productive conversations.

Another essential aspect of active listening is maintaining a non-interruptive behavior. It's natural to want to jump in and correct or argue, especially if you feel your child's viewpoints are misguided or incorrect. However, interrupting can escalate the conflict, particularly during a heated discussion. Allowing your child to express their thoughts without interruption conveys respect and worth, which can significantly reduce defensiveness and oppositional behavior. It shows them that their voice is valued, even if their behavior or attitude needs adjustment.

Lastly, questioning for clarity plays a significant role in active listening. This involves asking open-ended questions that prompt your child to elaborate on their thoughts and feelings. Questions like, "Can you tell me more about why you feel this way?" or "What would help you feel better right now?" encourage your child to express more deeply, providing you with further insight into their emotions and perspectives. These questions also signal to your child that you are genuinely interested in understanding them, not just controlling their behavior.

Interactive Element: Reflective Listening Exercise

Try this exercise to enhance your reflective listening skills:

1. Next time your child expresses a strong emotion, whether anger or sadness, resist the urge to give advice or solve the problem immediately.
2. Instead, repeat their words back to them, saying, "It sounds like you feel..."
3. Ask them to elaborate, "Can you explain why you feel that way?"
4. Observe their response and reflect on how this approach affects the conversation.

By integrating these active listening techniques into your daily interactions, you improve the quality of your conversations and model for your child how to listen and engage respectfully, skills that will benefit them in all areas of life.

2.2 THE ROLE OF BODY LANGUAGE IN COMMUNICATING WITH YOUR CHILD

When you think about communicating with your child, especially one who might be dealing with Oppositional Defiant Disorder (ODD), the focus often leans heavily toward what we say—choosing the right words and the right tone. However, body language is an equally crucial aspect of communication that might usually go unnoticed. Body language, or non-verbal communication, includes your gestures, posture, and facial expressions, and it can convey a lot about your emotions and intentions, sometimes even more powerfully than words. A clenched fist, a quick frown, or an averted gaze can speak volumes about your feelings and reactions, often subconsciously. This non-verbal communication layer can significantly impact how your child receives and interprets your messages.

For instance, consider a scenario where you are discussing school performance with your child. Even if your words are measured and encouraging, crossing your arms or maintaining a stern expression could signal disapproval or disappointment. Children, particularly those with ODD, who may be more sensitive to perceived criticism or confrontation, can react negatively to these cues, which might escalate the tension in what could have been a constructive conversation. Being mindful of your body language and learning to manage it can help create a more inviting and safe communication environment. This involves maintaining an open posture—uncrossed arms and legs, nodding while listening, and slightly leaning forward—these gestures show openness and willingness to engage without confrontation. Smiling, maintaining gentle eye contact, and nodding can reinforce the verbal message of support and understanding.

Mirroring, another powerful technique in non-verbal communication, involves subtly mimicking the positive body language of your child. If they are sitting in a relaxed manner, adopting a similar relaxed posture can enhance connection and empathy. Mirroring signals the child that you are in sync with them, which can be reassuring. It shows that you are engaged and attuned to their feelings. This doesn't mean copying every move—which can appear mocking—but instead capturing the essence of their posture or mood. For example, if your child is speaking animatedly about a topic they are passionate about, showing similar enthusiasm through your facial expressions and gestures can reinforce your interest and approval, enhancing the bond between you.

However, just as positive body language can build bridges, negative gestures can widen gaps. Certain types of body language, such as pointing fingers, rolling eyes, or sighing heavily, can escalate tensions or convey disapproval, anger, or frustration. For a child with ODD, who may already feel easily judged or opposed, these gestures can trigger defensive or more defiant reactions. Therefore, becoming conscious of and controlling such gestures during interactions is crucial. It helps to maintain a neutral facial expression and use softer, more open gestures that encourage rather than confront. Keeping your voice tone and facial expressions aligned with your positive intent can substantially affect how your message is received.

Understanding and refining your body language can transform the dynamics of your interactions. It's about aligning your non-verbal cues with your verbal messages to provide clear, consistent, and supportive communication. By being aware of and adjusting your body language, you avoid sending mixed signals and foster an atmosphere of openness and trust. This, in turn, encourages your child to be more open, less defensive, and more cooperative, paving the way for more effective and harmonious communication. By focusing on what you say and how you say it—through words and body language—you create a comprehensive communication strategy that can significantly improve your interactions and relationship with your child, especially in managing the complex challenges associated with ODD.

2.3 CONFLICT RESOLUTION TECHNIQUES THAT REALLY WORK

Navigating conflict with a child who has Oppositional Defiant Disorder (ODD) requires a thoughtful approach, where the timing and the environment play a crucial role in the outcome. Choosing the right moment and a neutral setting to address sensitive issues can make a significant difference. Engaging in a serious conversation right after an incident or in a place where a child feels cornered, like their own room, often leads to defensive reactions and can escalate conflicts rather than resolve them. Instead, selecting a quiet moment and a neutral setting, perhaps during a walk or a calm evening at home, sets a more open stage for dialogue. This strategy minimizes emotionally charged responses and helps the child feel more secure, making them more receptive to listening and engaging in meaningful conversation.

How parents express their feelings during these conversations also impacts the effectiveness of the communication. Using "I-statements" is a powerful tool in this regard. This technique involves framing your feelings and needs from your perspective without blaming or criticizing the child, which can significantly reduce their defensiveness. For example, instead of saying, "You never listen to me," you might say, "I feel frustrated when it seems like I'm not being heard." This slight shift in phrasing can change the dynamic of the interaction, as it expresses vulnerability and focuses on your feelings rather than placing blame. By modeling this communication style, you keep the lines of dialogue open and teach your child a healthier way to express their frustrations and needs.

Compromise and negotiation are further skills that can transform how conflicts are resolved in your household. These skills involve giving and taking that respects the needs and desires of both you and your child. For instance, if bedtime is a consistent battleground, a compromise might involve letting your child choose a book to read together, acknowledging their need for autonomy while still adhering to the bedtime routine. This approach fosters a sense of collaboration rather than confrontation. It shows your child that their opinions are valued and that conflict resolution can be a positive and constructive process. By involving your child in finding a middle ground, you also help them develop valuable problem-solving skills beyond the family environment.

Following through on agreements made during these discussions is critical to building trust and accountability. Sticking to this agreement is essential when both parties agree to a solution. If compromises are forgotten or dismissed, it can lead to feelings of betrayal or distrust, undermining future attempts at resolution. Consistency in follow-through shows your child that you are reliable and the agreements are taken seriously, reinforcing the importance of accountability on both sides. Whether it's a promise you've made to spend more time together or a behavioral change your child has agreed to, honoring these commitments is critical to maintaining a healthy, respectful relationship. This consistency helps manage the current conflict and sets a precedent for how future disagreements will be handled, establishing a pattern of reliability and respect that can significantly reduce the frequency and intensity of conflicts.

By integrating these conflict resolution techniques—choosing the right timing and setting, using I-stipulations, embracing compromise, and ensuring follow-through—you create a framework within which many of the challenges of parenting a child with ODD can be more effectively managed. This approach resolves individual disputes and teaches essential life skills, helping your child navigate a world where conflict is a part of human interaction. Through these strategies, you are working to solve the immediate challenges and investing in your child's long-term ability to engage with others respectfully and constructively.

2.4 USING VALIDATION TO BUILD EMPATHY

Validation is a powerful communication tool. It involves acknowledging and accepting your child's feelings and perspectives. This doesn't necessarily mean you agree with their feelings or words. Still, it does mean you recognize their emotions as valid and understandable within their personal context. For children, especially those with Oppositional Defiant Disorder (ODD), feeling understood is a cornerstone of emotional security and can significantly influence their behavior and self-esteem.

Understanding the importance of validation begins with recognizing that all emotions are valid. This is a crucial step in effective communication with your child. When a child expresses frustration or anger, the instinct might be to counter their feelings or correct their perspective, mainly if it seems irrational or overblown. However, validation starts with accepting that their emotions are real and impactful. For instance, if your child is upset over what seems like a minor change in plans, saying something like, "I see that you're really upset because we can't go to the park today as we planned," acknowledges their feelings without judgment. This approach does not indulge or reinforce negative behaviors but communicates that you are attuned to their feelings. Such validation can help de-escalate emotions, paving the way for more rational discussions about how to cope with disappointments and frustrations.

Using validating statements is a skill that can be learned and refined with practice. These statements should be specific to the feelings your child is expressing and can be as simple as "It sounds like you're feeling really disappointed" or "That seems like it was really embarrassing for you." These responses show that you are listening and empathizing with their experience. It's important to avoid generic or dismissive reactions like, "It's not a big deal" or "You'll get over it," which can feel invalidating to a child and often exacerbate the situation. Instead, reflecting back on what you hear from them validates their feelings. It helps them understand and label their emotions, a critical skill in emotional development.

The impact of regular validation on your relationship with your child can be profound. When children feel that their emotions are understood and respected, they are more likely to feel secure and supported. This emotional security can lead to fewer conflicts, as children are less likely to escalate their emotions to be heard. Moreover, validated children are more likely to develop empathy, understanding, and accepting the feelings of others. This can enhance their social interactions and relationships outside the family as well. Regular validation fosters an open line of communication in which your child feels safe to express their thoughts and feelings. This openness can transform your relationship, creating a more harmonious and supportive family environment.

However, it's also crucial to recognize and avoid invalidating responses, which can be subtle but damaging. Phrases like "You shouldn't feel that way" or "Why can't you be more like your sister?" dismiss the child's feelings and imply that their emotions are wrong or unworthy. These messages can erode self-esteem and trust, leading to more defensive and oppositional behavior. Teaching yourself to recognize these patterns in your communication and replacing them with validating alternatives is a fundamental step in supporting your child's emotional health. Instead of diminishing their feelings, try to understand the reason behind their emotions and communicate that understanding back to them. This doesn't mean you concede to unreasonable demands or behaviors. Still, you affirm their right to feel and express emotions, essential for healthy emotional development.

By embracing validation as a key communication strategy, you help your child navigate their emotions more effectively, building a foundation of empathy and understanding that supports their emotional and behavioral growth. This approach not only aids in managing the challenges associated with ODD but also enriches your relationship with your child, creating a more empathetic and connected family dynamic. Through consistent practice of validation, you foster an environment where emotions are handled with care and respect, setting the stage for your child to develop into a compassionate and self-aware individual.

2.5 AGE-APPROPRIATE COMMUNICATION TACTICS

As your child grows, how you communicate needs to evolve to match their developmental stage. This isn't just about making sure you're understood; it's about connecting in ways that respect their growing complexities. The way you talk to a preschooler, for instance, is vastly different from how you might approach a conversation with a teenager. Recognizing and adapting to these differences can significantly enhance the effectiveness of your interactions, especially when managing a child with Oppositional Defiant Disorder (ODD).

For younger children, simplification is critical but doesn't equate to talking down to them. Young minds are wonderfully curious and often more perceptive than they're given credit for. They respond well to clear, concrete language that reduces abstract concepts into tangible examples they encounter daily. For example, instead of abstractly explaining the importance of sharing, illustrate the idea through a story or a game that involves taking turns. Visual aids can also be incredibly effective at this stage.

Simple charts that track behaviors with corresponding rewards can clarify the rules and expectations, providing a visual reminder of what is expected and the positive outcomes of following those rules. This method helps manage behavior and makes communication about expectations clear and accessible for younger children.

When transitioning communication with teenagers, the approach shifts significantly. Teenagers are navigating a complex stage of development where they are forming their identities and craving more autonomy. Acknowledging their growing need for independence and respecting their viewpoints are crucial. When communicating with teenagers, especially those with ODD, it's essential to frame conversations in a way that respects their intelligence and autonomy. This might mean explaining the reasons behind rules rather than enforcing them 'because I said so.' Engage them in discussions about family decisions where appropriate, and listen genuinely to their input. When teenagers feel respected and valued, they are more likely to engage cooperatively.

Additionally, this stage of development is ideal for teaching more advanced conflict-resolution skills. Encourage your teenager to express their feelings using "I" statements, and model this behavior yourself. This not only helps resolve conflicts but also equips them with skills that will aid their social interactions outside the home.

In today's digital age, technology also plays a pivotal role in communication. While it's unrealistic—and not necessarily beneficial—to remove technology entirely, guiding its use can enhance rather than inhibit communication. For younger children, interactive apps that encourage learning through games can be a part of your communication strategy, especially for abstract concepts or where the child resists traditional teaching methods. For teenagers, leverage technology as a way to stay connected. Texting about their day or using apps to organize family schedules can keep lines of communication open. It's also an opportunity to teach responsible and respectful digital communication, setting guidelines that help them navigate online interactions safely and respectfully.

Navigating the changing landscape of your child's developmental stages requires flexibility and an understanding of their needs and capabilities at each stage. By tailoring your communication strategies to be age-appropriate, you foster a better understanding and a stronger connection with your child and support their growth into well-rounded individuals. This dynamic approach to communication is particularly crucial in managing and guiding a child with ODD, as it builds a foundation of trust and respect that can mitigate many behavioral challenges.

As this chapter closes, we reflect on the importance of evolving communication as our children grow. From using simple visual aids with young children to engaging in respectful, reasoned discussions with teenagers, your approach should adapt to meet your child's developmental needs. This adaptive communication fosters better behavior management in children with ODD and a stronger, more connected relationship with them. The next chapter will delve into behavioral management techniques as we move forward, building on the communication foundations we've set to equip you with practical strategies for managing and guiding your child's behavior.

CHAPTER 3
PRACTICAL BEHAVIOR MANAGEMENT TECHNIQUES

When dealing with Oppositional Defiant Disorder (ODD), understanding and implementing effective behavior management strategies can feel like navigating a complex maze. Each turn and corner presents its own set of challenges and learning opportunities. This chapter aims to provide practical, clear, and effective tools to guide your child toward better behavior patterns using a compassionate and structured approach. Let's explore how positive reinforcement and well-designed reward systems can create significant, positive changes in your family dynamics, enhancing both your parenting experience and your child's developmental journey.

3.1 POSITIVE REINFORCEMENT AND REWARD SYSTEMS

Understanding Positive Reinforcement

Positive reinforcement is a strategy used to encourage a desired behavior by rewarding it immediately after it occurs, thus increasing the likelihood of the behavior recurring. This technique is grounded in behavioral psychology and has proven effective, especially in children with behavioral challenges such as ODD. The key here is to distinguish between rewards and bribes; the former is given after a desired behavior to reinforce it, while the latter is offered in advance to coax the child into acting a certain way. For instance, rewarding your child with praise after they have completed their homework reinforces the behavior for the next time, whereas offering them a treat beforehand to get them to do their homework can lead to dependency and manipulation.

Designing Effective Reward Systems

Creating a reward system that resonates with your child involves understanding what motivates them. This system should include tangible rewards, like small toys or special treats, and intangible rewards, such as praise, extra bedtime stories, or more one-on-one time with you. For example, if your child loves comics, allowing them extra reading time as a reward for positive behavior can be highly effective. Similarly, praising their effort and progress can boost their self-esteem and reinforce good behavior. The rewards must be appealing and sustainable; they should be easy to consistently implement and ideally encourage further positive activities.

Timing and Consistency

The effectiveness of a reward system hinges significantly on the timing and consistency of the reinforcement. Immediate rewards help the child make a clear connection between their behavior and the positive outcome, solidifying the learning of the desired behavior. Consistency in applying these rewards whenever the behavior occurs is just as crucial. Inconsistent rewards can create confusion and unpredictability, making behavior management less effective. For instance, if a child is rewarded with extra playtime each time they tidy up their room without being prompted, they are more likely to repeat this behavior if the reward is consistent.

Evaluating and Adjusting the System

As with any strategy, it's essential to monitor the effectiveness of your reward system and make adjustments as necessary. This ensures the system remains motivating for the child and practical for the family. Regularly check in with your child to gauge their interest in the rewards. Are they still motivated by them? Do the rewards encourage further positive behavior? Sometimes, what worked well for a month may become less enticing as the child's interests and motivations evolve. Adjusting the rewards to fit their developing interests or increasing the challenge as their behavior improves can help maintain the system's effectiveness. For example, if your child consistently shows good behavior in completing homework on time, raising the bar slightly by adding a small extra task might be appropriate, with greater rewards.

Interactive Element: Reward System Tracker

Consider implementing a simple tracker for both you and your child to monitor the rewards system's effectiveness:

- Create a chart that lists the behaviors to be reinforced alongside the corresponding rewards.
- Each time the desired behavior is displayed, mark it on the chart.
- Have weekly reviews with your child to discuss the chart, celebrate successes, and discuss any adjustments to the rewards or behaviors.

This visual and interactive element helps you keep track of progress and involves your child in the process, making it a collaborative effort to manage their behavior. It's a practical tool that adds structure and clarity to the reinforcement process, helping you and your child see the tangible outcomes of consistent positive behavior.

Understanding and implementing these strategies within your family dynamics can create a supportive environment that encourages and rewards positive behavior. This approach helps manage the challenges associated with ODD. It fosters a relationship based on understanding and mutual respect, which is crucial for your child's overall growth and well-being. As we explore other practical behavioral management techniques, remember that each strategy builds upon these foundations to create a more harmonious and supportive family environment.

3.2 ESTABLISHING AND MAINTAINING CONSISTENT ROUTINES

For children grappling with Oppositional Defiant Disorder (ODD), the world can often seem like an unpredictable and confusing place where even minor deviations from what they anticipate can trigger intense reactions. This is why establishing and maintaining consistent routines is beneficial and essential. Routines provide a structure that can make the world more predictable and less threatening. Children with ODD find comfort in knowing what to expect; it reduces their anxiety and the need to fight against what comes next. This predictability helps them manage their reactions to daily demands, reducing instances of defiance that often stem from an inability to handle unexpected changes or unclear expectations.

When setting up routines, involving your child in the process is crucial. This inclusion increases their sense of control and ownership, making them more likely to adhere to the routine. Start by discussing the benefits of having a routine with your child. Explain how a routine will help them manage their day better and give them more time for enjoyable activities. Once they understand the benefits, collaborate on creating a routine that works for both of you. For instance, let them choose between doing homework before or after a snack. This small choice can significantly affect how they perceive and cooperate with the daily schedule.

Next, break down the day into manageable segments. For a school day, the routine might include getting ready in the morning, attending school, doing homework, having playtime, eating dinner, and preparing for bed. Work with your child to set a time frame for each activity. Use positive language and frame each part of the routine as something they get to do rather than have to do. For example, instead of saying, "You have to do your homework," you might say, "You get to complete your homework now, so the rest of the evening is free for fun!"

Incorporating visual aids can significantly enhance understanding and compliance, especially for younger children or visual learners. Visual aids like charts, calendars, or digital reminders serve as cues that can help reinforce routines and make them easier to follow. Consider creating a visual schedule that depicts different parts of the day with simple icons or pictures. Place this schedule in a common area like the kitchen or your child's bedroom where it's easily visible. This constant visual reminder can help them internalize and stick to the routine more independently over time.

Handling disruptions is an inevitable part of life, and for children with ODD, how these disruptions are managed can significantly impact their behavior. Disruptions like holidays, weekends, or unexpected events can unsettle the established routine. When such disruptions occur, try to maintain as much of the routine as possible. For example, if bedtime is usually at 8 PM, keep to that time even during holidays. If an unexpected event disrupts the day, communicate this change to your child as soon as possible. Explain why the routine is changing and the new plan, ensuring you reaffirm when the usual routine will resume.

When reintroducing the usual routine after a disruption, do so gradually and with empathy. Acknowledge that adjusting back to the routine might be challenging and offer support through this transition. For instance, if your child has stayed up late over vacation, gradually adjust their bedtime by 15 minutes earlier each night until you're back to the usual time. Always pair these adjustments with lots of positive reinforcement for each step they successfully take towards normalizing the routine.

Establishing and maintaining a consistent routine creates a sense of security and predictability and fosters an environment where your child can thrive despite the challenges of ODD. The structure provided by a routine can be a comforting, stabilizing force in their lives, reducing anxiety and defiant behaviors. By involving your child in creating their routine and using tools like visual aids to reinforce it, you empower them to manage their day better and gradually build the independence and resilience needed to navigate daily life more smoothly.

3.3 CONSEQUENCES VS. PUNISHMENT: A BALANCED APPROACH

When navigating the complex terrain of behavior management, especially for children with Oppositional Defiant Disorder (ODD), understanding the distinction between consequences and punishment can significantly influence your approach and, ultimately, the outcomes. Consequences are natural or logical responses to behavior that help teach responsibility and accountability. They are inherently connected to the child's actions and are designed to encourage reflection and learning. For example, suppose a child neglects to complete their homework. In that case, a natural consequence might be receiving a lower grade, directly correlating with their action. Punishment, on the other hand, often involves imposing a penalty that might not be directly related to the behavior, such as revoking TV privileges for a week due to poor performance at school. This approach can breed resentment and defiance, as the child might fail to see a logical link between their behavior and the punishment.

Implementing logical consequences effectively requires a thoughtful approach where the connection between actions and outcomes is clear and reasonable. This is crucial in helping the child understand the impact of their decisions and behaviors. To establish logical consequences, start by ensuring the consequences are directly related to the behavior. For instance, if a child makes a mess while playing, a logical consequence would be to involve them in the cleanup process. This not only teaches them about responsibility but also about the natural outcomes of their actions. Discussing these consequences with your child beforehand is important so they understand the potential results of their choices. This clarity helps them see these consequences as fair and be more accepting of them when applied.

However, there are pitfalls you should be cautious to avoid. One common mistake is implementing overly harsh or unrelated penalties, which can be perceived as unfair by the child, leading to increased resistance and behavioral problems. For example, canceling a weekend outing because of a minor misbehavior at dinner might seem disproportionate, unrelated, confusing, and frustrating to the child. Another pitfall is delayed consequences. When too much time passes between the behavior and the consequence, the connection gets blurred, and the lesson is lost. Consistency is another cornerstone of effective behavioral management. Inconsistencies in applying consequences can undermine their effectiveness, leading to confusion and insecurity, which can exacerbate behavioral issues in children with ODD.

Empowering children through choice within boundaries is another powerful strategy that can reduce resistance and enhance cooperation. This involves providing limited decisions that lead to positive outcomes. For example, offer your child the choice between doing their homework before dinner or after dinner. Either option leads to the desired behavior—completing homework—while giving the child a sense of control over their actions. This approach reduces power struggles as children feel more autonomous and involved in managing their behavior. It's a way of setting boundaries that guide positive behavior while respecting the child's need for some control over their environment, which is especially important for those with ODD who often feel a need to resist authority.

By integrating these strategies—distinguishing between consequences and punishment, implementing logical consequences, avoiding common pitfalls, and empowering through choice—you create a balanced approach to behavior management. This approach addresses the symptoms of ODD and fosters an environment of understanding and respect, which is essential for the child's growth and development. Through these methods, you not only manage behavior effectively but also teach valuable life lessons about responsibility, consequences, and the importance of making thoughtful choices. This helps in the immediate management of ODD and equips your child with the tools to navigate their world more successfully, fostering a sense of competence and confidence that extends beyond the home into every area of their life.

3.4 DE-ESCALATING TECHNIQUES DURING OUTBURSTS

Handling outbursts from a child with Oppositional Defiant Disorder (ODD) can be one of the most challenging aspects of parenting. These episodes can escalate quickly and test your patience and emotional resilience. However, with the right strategies, you can learn to de-escalate these situations effectively, helping your child regain control of their emotions and behavior. The key is understanding the triggers, remaining composed, and employing verbal and physical techniques to soothe rather than inflame the situation.

Identifying what triggers your child's outbursts is the first critical step in preventing and managing these intense reactions. Triggers can vary widely but often include changes in routine, feelings of frustration, sensory overload, or perceived injustice. Observing your child's behavior patterns can help you predict and preempt potential outbursts. For instance, if your child tends to have tantrums after school, it might be due to a combination of tiredness and the need to process a day's worth of social and academic stimulation. By recognizing these patterns, you can intervene early, perhaps by providing a quiet, calm space immediately after school to help them decompress.

Once an outburst begins, the importance of your response cannot be overstated. Staying calm and composed might be challenging, but it is crucial as it sets the tone for the interaction. Children often mirror the emotional state of their caregivers. The situation will likely escalate if you respond with visible stress or agitation. Instead, strive to maintain a calm demeanor. Use a soft, steady tone of voice and relaxed body language to convey to your child that you are in control and there to support them.

Effective communication during these moments involves specific phrases and tones that acknowledge your child's feelings and guide them toward calming down. Phrases like, "I see you're really upset right now, and that's okay," validate their feelings and can help diffuse the intensity. Follow this by gently guiding them with options to calm down, such as, "Let's take a few deep breaths together," or "Would you like to sit in your quiet space with your favorite book?" These suggestions offer constructive alternatives and give your child a sense of choice in the matter, which can be particularly empowering for children who often feel they lack control over their environment.

Physical strategies also play a significant role in managing outbursts. For some children, engaging in physical activity can be an effective way to dispel anger or frustration. Activities like squeezing a stress ball, jumping on a trampoline, or even tearing up scrap paper can provide a physical outlet for their emotions. For others, gentle, comforting touches such as a hand on the shoulder or a hug (if the child is receptive) can be soothing. Additionally, guiding your child to a predetermined 'calm down' space where they can feel safe and relax away from external stimuli can be beneficial. This space should be a comforting environment, with soft pillows, favorite toys, or calming music, where they can retreat until they feel better able to handle their emotions.

Implementing these techniques requires patience and consistency, but over time, they can significantly reduce the frequency and intensity of outbursts. By providing your child with the tools and support they need to manage their emotions effectively, you are not only helping to de-escalate difficult situations but also teaching them valuable self-regulation skills that will serve them well throughout life.

As we close this chapter on practical behavior management techniques, we reflect on the importance of understanding and addressing the unique challenges presented by ODD. From establishing positive reinforcement systems and consistent routines to differentiating between consequences and punishment and mastering the art of de-escalation, each strategy plays a pivotal role in fostering a supportive and nurturing environment. These approaches pave the way for more peaceful interactions and a deeper understanding between you and your child, setting the stage for the next chapter, where we will explore strategies for handling everyday challenges with your child.

CHAPTER 4
HANDLING EVERYDAY CHALLENGES

Navigating the daily life of a parent can be akin to steering a ship through uncharted waters. Every day brings new challenges and opportunities for growth. When your child struggles with Oppositional Defiant Disorder (ODD), these regular parental challenges can often amplify, turning routine tasks into significant hurdles. Understanding how to manage these everyday situations effectively is crucial not only for your child's development but also for maintaining a harmonious family environment. This chapter delves into practical strategies that can transform potentially tumultuous mornings into a smoother start to the day, setting a positive tone for you and your child.

4.1 MORNING ROUTINES WITHOUT THE BATTLE

Structured Morning Plans

Mornings can often set the tone for the entire day. For children with ODD, a predictable morning routine is vital as it diminishes anxiety and reduces resistance to the day's tasks. Establishing a structured morning routine helps your child understand what to expect each day, which can significantly lower morning stress levels for everyone involved. The key is consistency and predictability—two elements that can transform chaotic mornings into calm ones.

Start by mapping out each morning activity, from waking up to leaving the house. This schedule should be discussed and visually displayed on a chart or a whiteboard for your child in a common area like the kitchen. Each part of the routine should have a specific time slot, from brushing teeth to packing the school bag. Over time, this consistency helps embed these activities into your child's mental landscape, making resistance less likely as the routine becomes a regular part of their expectations.

Preparation and Organization

Preparation is a crucial element that can make mornings far less stressful. Encourage your child to prepare for the next day the night before. This can include laying out clothes, packing the school bag, preparing lunch, and setting out any necessary items for morning activities. Involve your child in these preparations to give them a sense of control and responsibility.

For younger children, you might use a checklist with pictures that show the tasks they need to complete before bed. Encourage older children to list what they need for the next day and check off each item as they prepare. This ensures they have everything ready and helps instill a habit of organization and foresight, which are valuable life skills.

Incentives for Cooperation

Incentives can be a powerful tool for encouraging cooperation in children with ODD. These should be small, simple rewards that come immediately after the desired behavior, reinforcing the connection between positive action and positive outcome. For instance, if your child manages to get ready on time without a fuss, they might earn extra storytime in the evening or their choice of breakfast on the weekend. These incentives should be clearly outlined beforehand and consistently applied to be effective.

It is important to choose incentives that are meaningful to your child and manageable for you. They should be easy to incorporate into your daily routine without causing extra stress. Remember, the goal is to make mornings easier, not to add more complexity to your day.

Role of Calm Parental Guidance

Your role in the morning routine is the most crucial. Children often take emotional cues from their parents, and your mood and behavior in the morning can influence theirs. Strive to remain calm and patient, even when things don't go as planned. Your calmness not only helps de-escalate potential conflicts but also models the kind of behavior you want to see in your child.

Set a positive tone by engaging in pleasant conversation, discussing the plans for the day, or something your child looks forward to. This can shift their focus from the mundane aspects of getting ready to the more exciting parts of their day. If tensions start to rise, take a moment to breathe deeply and remind yourself of the bigger picture—the goal is not just to get through the morning but to do so in a way that supports your child's emotional and behavioral growth.

Implementing these strategies may take time to change things, but your mornings can become significantly smoother with consistency and patience. These approaches help manage the practical aspects of starting the day and foster an environment of understanding and support, setting a positive tone that carries through the rest of the day.

4.2 MANAGING PUBLIC OUTBURSTS

Navigating the complexities of parenting a child with Oppositional Defiant Disorder (ODD) often involves handling unexpected outbursts, which can be particularly challenging when they occur in public settings. These situations not only test your patience and adaptive skills but also place you under the scrutiny of onlookers, adding an extra layer of stress. Effective management of these incidents starts well before the actual outburst through careful anticipation and planning. Understanding your child's triggers is key—common triggers might include crowded environments, changes in routine, or sensory overload. By identifying what specifically sets off your child, you can better anticipate challenging situations and plan accordingly.

Preparation might involve:

- Discussing the outing ahead of time with your child.
- Setting clear expectations.
- Planning together how to handle potential stress.

For instance, if you know that a busy supermarket can overwhelm your child, you might decide together on a signal they can give you when they feel overwhelmed, which could cue a break or a change in activity. You can also plan for less crowded times or even involve them in a game that focuses their attention away from the chaos. Another helpful strategy is having a "safety plan" that could include a quiet spot where you can both retreat if things become too intense. This helps manage the situation and empowers your child by involving them in the solution.

When an outburst does occur, the strategies for immediate response are crucial. First and foremost is maintaining your calm. This can be challenging under the eyes of bystanders, but remember, your primary audience is your child. Using a calm, quiet voice can help counteract the intensity of their emotions and prevent the situation from escalating. Distraction techniques can also be very effective. This could mean shifting your child's attention to a more calming focus, like pointing out different items around them and asking them to describe them, or even a quick, engaging game or activity you've prepared in advance. Taking a brief timeout by stepping away from the triggering environment can also help if feasible. This might mean going to a less crowded part of a store or stepping outside for a few minutes.

Following the incident, it's important to discuss the outburst with your child to reflect on what happened and how it can be handled differently in the future. Choose a time when both you and your child are calm. Discuss what each of you noticed, what you felt, and how you might better prepare for next time. This not only helps in understanding the triggers more profoundly but also aids in developing your child's self-awareness and self-regulation skills. It's also a comforting assurance that they can learn and grow from these experiences rather than just being punished for them.

Educating bystanders is another aspect that, while often overlooked, can significantly impact your experience. Not everyone understands ODD and its challenges; facing judgment can be an additional stressor. You can carry small informational cards about ODD that you can hand out to people who express concern or curiosity. Alternatively, a simple explanation that your child is dealing with a challenge and you are handling it can suffice. This helps manage social expectations and raises awareness about ODD, which can lead to greater understanding and support from the community.

Handling public outbursts requires patience, preparation, and a lot of empathy. You can manage these challenging situations by anticipating potential triggers and planning how to address them, maintaining calm during incidents, and using them as learning opportunities afterward. Moreover, by educating those around you, you make the moment easier for yourself and your child and contribute to a more understanding and inclusive society.

4.3 DEALING WITH SCHOOL-RELATED ISSUES

Navigating the educational landscape when your child has Oppositional Defiant Disorder (ODD) can often feel like walking a tightrope—balancing your child's needs with school expectations and policies. Effective communication with school staff is not just helpful; it's crucial. It ensures that you stay informed about your child's day-to-day behavior and any incidents, which can provide insights into potential triggers and effective strategies. Regular communication might mean setting up a weekly or bi-weekly check-in with your child's teacher or having a direct line to the school counselor. During these conversations, it's essential to ask specific questions about your child's social interactions, responses to authority, and any situations that might have escalated during school hours. This helps you stay proactive in managing your child's behavior and builds a bridge of trust and cooperation with the school staff, showing that you are an engaged and concerned parent working towards the best outcomes for your child.

Participation in developing and adjusting your child's behavioral plans at school is also a key area where your involvement can make a significant difference. Behavioral plans are structured strategies schools use to help students manage their behavior to promote learning and social interaction while minimizing disruptions. As a parent, advocating for a plan that mirrors the strategies used at home can provide consistency, which is often crucial for children with ODD. For instance, if a certain consequence or reward system works well at home, suggesting its incorporation into your child's school behavioral plan can help maintain a sense of familiarity and structure for your child, reducing confusion and mixed signals. Participate actively in the planning meetings, offering insights into what has been effective in other settings and being open to suggestions from educational professionals who might have additional expertise.

Preparing for school meetings is another area where focused effort can pay off. These meetings can sometimes feel daunting as you navigate discussions about your child's needs and school policies. To ensure that you are fully prepared, start by documenting any relevant behaviors, incidents, and the effectiveness of current strategies. Keeping a log can be incredibly helpful, providing a clear record that can be referred to during the meeting. Also, prepare a list of questions or concerns you have about the school's approach or policies related to managing ODD. This might include queries about the potential for academic accommodations, the availability of special education services, or how discipline is handled for children with behavioral disorders. By attending meetings well-prepared, you can ensure that the discussion is productive and focused on finding the best solutions for your child.

Interactive Element: Checklist for School Meeting Preparation

- Behavior and Incident Log: Keep a detailed record of dates, behavior descriptions, and any school incidents.
- Practical Strategies: Note which strategies work at home and could be integrated into the school plan.
- Questions List: Write down all questions regarding school policies, additional support services, or specific incidents that need discussion.
- Goals for the Meeting: Set clear objectives for what you hope to achieve, such as updating a behavioral plan or discussing additional resources.

Finally, creating a support system within the school can significantly enhance your child's educational experience. This involves building relationships with teachers and school counselors, special education professionals, and even administrators. These professionals can offer additional support and resources to help manage your child's behavior more effectively. For example, school counselors can provide one-on-one sessions with your child to work through social or emotional challenges, while special education professionals might offer insights into instructional strategies that are more effective for students with ODD. Collaborating closely with these professionals helps tailor the educational approach to your child's needs. It ensures that they have a support network within the school, creating a community that fosters academic and personal growth.

By taking these steps—engaging in effective communication, participating actively in behavioral planning, preparing thoroughly for school meetings, and collaborating to build a strong support network—you can help create an educational environment that is both supportive and effective for your child. This proactive approach addresses the challenges associated with ODD. It promotes an atmosphere of understanding and adaptation that can significantly impact your child's ability to succeed and thrive in the school setting.

4.4 HANDLING DISRESPECT AND AGGRESSION AT HOME

When your home becomes the stage for displays of disrespect or aggression, especially from a child struggling with Oppositional Defiant Disorder (ODD), the atmosphere can quickly become charged with tension. It's crucial to approach these situations with strategies that address the immediate behavior and contribute to a long-term solution. Managing these moments effectively hinges on remaining composed, modeling respectful behavior, and applying appropriate consequences.

Immediate Calming Techniques

Staying calm yourself is the first and possibly the most challenging step when facing disrespect or aggression. Techniques such as taking deep breaths or pausing before you respond can be beneficial. Deep breathing helps in regulating your emotions and lowers your stress response, making it easier to handle the situation with a clearer mind. Similarly, pausing before reacting gives you time to collect your thoughts and approach the response more strategically rather than impulsively. You might count to ten in your mind or use a brief mantra to center yourself, such as "Stay calm, respond wisely." This moment of pause is often all it takes to shift from a potential escalation to a more controlled interaction.

Setting Clear Consequences

Clear, immediate, and appropriate consequences are essential in teaching children about the impact of their behavior. The key here is consistency and immediacy, which help reinforce the connection between behavior and consequence. Consequences should be directly related to the behavior and should be explained to the child in a straightforward manner. For instance, if a child reacts aggressively during a disagreement, a consequence might be losing the privilege to watch their favorite show later. Communicating this consequence calmly and clearly is essential, as well as ensuring the child understands why their behavior led to this outcome. Equally important is following through on the consequence; inconsistency can weaken the effectiveness of your strategy and send mixed signals to your child.

Teaching Respect Through Modeling

Modeling the behavior you expect from your child is one of the most powerful tools at your disposal. Children learn significantly from observing how adults, particularly their parents, behave. By treating everyone in the household with respect, even in challenging situations, you set a standard for how to interact with others. This includes using polite language, listening actively when others speak, and handling disagreements calmly and respectfully. Demonstrating these behaviors consistently helps your child understand what respect looks like in practice and emphasizes that disrespectful behavior is unacceptable.

Use of De-escalation Strategies

De-escalation strategies are crucial in reducing the intensity of an aggressive or disrespectful encounter. Techniques such as lowering your voice, changing the environment, or offering choices can be effective. Speaking in a low, calm tone can help soothe the situation, as high-pitched or loud voices might increase agitation. Changing the environment can help reset the mood; moving to another room or going outside for a few minutes might provide the necessary change in dynamics. Offering choices is another effective strategy, as it gives the child some control over the situation. For example, suppose a conflict arises over cleaning up toys. In that case, you might offer a choice between doing it now or after a five-minute break. These choices should lead to positive outcomes, reinforcing that respectful cooperation is more rewarding than conflict.

Implementing these strategies requires patience and practice, but they can significantly improve how you handle disrespect and aggression in your home. By maintaining your composure, setting clear and immediate consequences, modeling respectful behavior, and employing de-escalation techniques, you create an environment where respectful interactions are the norm and aggression is systematically and effectively managed. This not only helps resolve conflicts but also teaches your child valuable skills in managing their emotions and behaviors respectfully and constructively.

4.5 STRATEGIES FOR BEDTIME RESISTANCE

Navigating bedtime with a child who has Oppositional Defiant Disorder (ODD) can often transform what should be a peaceful end to the day into a battleground. The resistance to bedtime routines can stem from various factors, including a child's need for control, anxiety, or simply the day's accumulated frustrations. Establishing a consistent bedtime routine is vital to ease this transition and foster an environment conducive to sleep. This routine acts as a signal, informing your child that the day is winding down and it's time to prepare for sleep. Including calming activities such as reading a book together, listening to gentle music, or engaging in quiet play can significantly help in this transition. These activities should be predictable and enjoyable, creating a positive and calm end to the day.

Creating an environment conducive to sleep is equally important. The bedroom should be a haven of comfort and tranquility. Using blackout curtains to block out any external light can help signal to your child's body that it's time to wind down, enhancing their natural sleep rhythms. The choice of bedding can also play a role; ensure that it is comfortable and appropriate for the season, avoiding anything that might cause discomfort or disruption during the night. Perhaps most crucial is the removal of stimulating electronics from the bedroom. Devices such as tablets, phones, and even televisions can interfere with the brain's ability to relax due to the blue light emitted from screens, which suppresses the natural production of melatonin, a hormone critical for sleep.

Addressing bedtime fears and anxieties is another critical component. Many children with ODD also experience heightened anxiety, which can make bedtime particularly stressful. Strategies to alleviate these fears can include using a night light or having a unique 'security' object like a stuffed animal that they can cuddle as they sleep. Additionally, teaching your child relaxation techniques such as deep breathing exercises or guided imagery can empower them to manage their anxiety independently. These techniques not only assist in creating a calm atmosphere but also give your child practical tools to help control their emotional responses.

Procrastination tactics are a common challenge that many parents face at bedtime, especially with children who have ODD. These tactics often manifest as repeated requests for water, additional stories, or one more game. Setting clear limits and sticking to them is crucial in managing these delaying strategies. This might involve establishing a clear and agreed-upon number of stories before bed or setting a specific 'lights out' time. Consistency is vital; once these limits are set, they should be adhered to strictly to avoid setting a precedent that such tactics can extend bedtime. Clear and consistent communication about these boundaries, delivered in a calm and understanding manner, helps reinforce the structure of the bedtime routine and reduces the likelihood of resistance.

Managing bedtime resistance effectively not only ensures a smoother end to the day but also contributes to the overall well-being of your child by fostering better sleep habits. This structured approach to bedtime, through routine, environment, addressing anxieties, and managing procrastination, creates a framework within which your child can find comfort and predictability. It's a crucial part of ending the day well and setting the tone for a new day ahead, ensuring your child is rested and ready for the challenges and growth opportunities that come with each morning.

As this chapter concludes, we reflect on the essential strategies discussed that help manage the everyday challenges you might face with a child who has ODD. From transforming morning routines into cooperative starts, handling public outbursts with calm precision, navigating school-related issues with proactive communication, to managing disrespect and aggression at home with clear consequences and respect. Each strategy is designed not just to address the immediate challenges but to foster an environment of understanding, respect, and routine that can significantly ease the daily stresses associated with raising a child with ODD.

Looking ahead, the next chapter will delve into the critical role of building positive family relationships. This foundation is about improving behavior and deepening connections within the family, creating a supportive network that celebrates each member's growth and contributions. Join me as we explore how strengthening these bonds can be pivotal in managing ODD and enhancing the overall quality of family life.

CHAPTER 5
BUILDING POSITIVE FAMILY RELATIONSHIPS

Navigating the complexities of raising a child with Oppositional Defiant Disorder (ODD) can often feel like trying to solve a puzzle with ever-shifting pieces. Amidst these challenges, building and maintaining strong family relationships can sometimes take a back seat. However, forging these positive connections is not just beneficial; it's essential for the emotional and psychological well-being of both you and your child. This chapter focuses on daily practices that can strengthen the bonds within your family, turning everyday interactions into opportunities for growth and connection.

5.1 DAILY PRACTICES TO STRENGTHEN PARENT-CHILD CONNECTIONS

Establish Daily Check-Ins

Imagine starting a tradition where, at the end of each day, you and your child spend a few quiet moments together discussing the day's events. This routine, known as daily check-ins, can significantly enhance your relationship with your child. These moments provide a safe space for your child to express their thoughts and feelings and for you to listen actively and empathetically. During these check-ins, encourage your child to share not just the highs of their day but also any lows or challenges they encountered. This practice helps you stay connected to your child's daily life and teaches them the invaluable skills of reflection and emotional expression. Over time, these daily check-ins can become a cherished routine that you and your child look forward to, fostering a deeper understanding and bond between you.

Incorporate Teamwork Activities

Teamwork activities are a fantastic way to enhance family bonding and teach children the importance of cooperation and mutual support. Engaging in tasks requiring teamwork, such as cooking a family meal or collaborating on a home improvement project, provides practical opportunities for everyone to work towards a common goal. These activities make mundane tasks more enjoyable and allow family members to rely on and learn from each other. These positive teamwork experiences can be particularly therapeutic for a child with ODD, as they help inculcate a sense of belonging and achievement. Moreover, sharing the responsibilities and joys of a completed task can reinforce the values of hard work and cooperation, essential skills for any child's development.

Use of Affirmations

Affirmations are powerful tools that can help bolster a child's self-esteem and promote positive self-perception, which is especially important for children with ODD who often struggle with feelings of inadequacy or negativity. Regularly affirming your child's efforts, rather than just the outcomes, helps them understand that their value does not solely lie in "success" but in the effort and perseverance they show. Phrases like "I'm really proud of how hard you tried" or "I love how you helped your sister with her homework" focus on the qualities behind the action, such as persistence, kindness, and dedication. These affirmations should be genuine and reflective of real efforts made by your child, as insincerity can be easily detected and might backfire. Integrating affirmations into your daily interactions can help shift the focus from what's going wrong to what's going right, fostering a more positive atmosphere at home.

Maintain Consistency in Interactions

Consistency in how you interact with your child lays a foundation of trust and security, which is crucial for children with ODD. They often feel more secure and less inclined to act out when they know what to expect from their parents. Consistency in your responses helps mitigate this uncertainty. For example, if a rule in your household is to have no screen time during meals, this should be consistently upheld. Similarly, your responses to certain behaviors should not fluctuate based on your mood; they should be predictable and reasoned. This consistency reduces confusion and helps your child understand the consequences of their actions more clearly, making them feel more secure and less compelled to test boundaries.

Through these practices, you can fortify the relationships within your family, creating a supportive and nurturing environment that not only meets the challenges of ODD but also enhances the quality of life for all family members. Each interaction, whether a daily check-in or a collaborative project, is an opportunity to reinforce these ties, building a resilient family dynamic that can withstand the challenges and celebrate the successes together.

5.2 POSITIVE REINFORCEMENT TECHNIQUES THAT ACTUALLY WORK

In the realm of parenting a child with Oppositional Defiant Disorder (ODD), the art of positive reinforcement is a valuable tool that can encourage desirable behaviors and foster a supportive family environment. One of the most effective forms of positive reinforcement is the use of specific praise. Unlike general praise, which might include vague comments like "good job," specific praise focuses on particular behaviors, making it clear to your child exactly what they did right. For example, instead of saying, "You're a good boy," you might say, "I really appreciate how you asked for help when you needed it today." This type of feedback helps your child understand which behaviors are valued and encourages them to repeat those actions. It also adds a layer of sincerity to your praise, as it shows you are paying attention to their efforts and challenges.

Implementing effective reward systems is another cornerstone of positive reinforcement that can motivate children with ODD by making the outcomes of their excellent behavior tangible and rewarding. Designing a reward system that resonates with your child involves understanding their interests and what motivates them most. A point system, for instance, can be particularly effective. In this system, specific positive behaviors are assigned a point value, and points can be accumulated and exchanged for privileges or small rewards. This could range from extra screen time to a special outing with a parent. The key to success with a reward system lies in its consistency and the immediacy of the reward following the desired behavior. Immediate rewards help solidify the connection between the behavior and the positive reinforcement, making the behavior more likely to be repeated.

The concept of natural consequences is another facet of positive reinforcement that can be instrumental in teaching children about the impact of their choices. Natural consequences naturally follow a specific behavior without the need for parental enforcement. For example, if a child refuses to wear a coat on a cold day, the natural consequence might be that they feel cold outside. Experiencing these outcomes can teach children that their choices have direct impacts, fostering a deeper understanding of cause and effect and encouraging them to make decisions that will have positive outcomes in the future. It's essential, however, to ensure that natural consequences are safe and not overly punitive, as the goal is to encourage learning and growth, not to cause distress or harm.

Consistency in the application of positive reinforcement strategies cannot be overstated. It is the glue that holds these techniques together and ensures their effectiveness. Whether it's the application of specific praise, the accrual of points in a reward system, or understanding natural consequences, consistency helps create a predictable environment where children with ODD can thrive. It reduces ambiguity and confusion and reinforces the learning of positive behaviors. When children understand that positive behaviors consistently result in positive feedback, they are more likely to adopt these behaviors in their daily lives, leading to improvements in family dynamics and personal development.

By incorporating these techniques into your parenting approach, you create a framework within which your child can learn and grow. Positive reinforcement promotes desirable behaviors and helps build a relationship based on mutual respect and understanding, which is particularly crucial in families navigating the challenges of ODD. Through specific praise, thoughtfully designed reward systems, the judicious use of natural consequences, and a commitment to consistency, you can foster an environment where positive behaviors are recognized, encouraged, and become the norm, paving the way for lasting change and harmonious family life.

5.3 THE ROLE OF QUALITY TIME IN BUILDING TRUST

Investing in regular, scheduled one-on-one time with each child is more than just a pleasant activity—it's a fundamental building block for nurturing trust and deepening your connection. This quality time, when thoughtfully planned and consistently prioritized, becomes a cornerstone of your relationship, offering a safe space where your child feels valued and heard. During these moments, engaging in activities your child enjoys can significantly enhance their sense of security and belonging. For example, if your child has a passion for painting, scheduling regular painting sessions together not only supports their interest but also shows that you value their passions. This investment goes a long way in building their confidence and trust in you.

These sessions also provide an excellent opportunity to introduce new activities that can broaden your child's experiences and learning. Whether exploring a new hobby together or simply going for a walk in a different part of town, these shared experiences can stimulate conversation and mutual discovery. The key is to keep these activities light and enjoyable, focusing on the experience and connection rather than achieving any specific outcome. This approach helps to reinforce the idea that the time spent together is about the relationship, not about the activity itself.

Active participation in your child's hobbies and interests plays a crucial role in strengthening this bond. Showing genuine interest and involvement in your child's values demonstrates your commitment to their happiness and well-being. This might mean learning more about their favorite video game, reading books on subjects they love, or even participating in classes or workshops together. By actively engaging in their world, you send a powerful message that their interests matter to you, which can enhance their self-esteem and the trust they place in you.

Furthermore, the conversations that unfold during these shared activities are invaluable. They offer natural opportunities for open dialogues about various topics, including life, dreams, and day-to-day challenges. These discussions are essential for building a solid communicative relationship where your child feels comfortable sharing their thoughts and feelings. This openness is vital for children with ODD, who may often feel misunderstood or judged. You are laying a foundation for stronger, more resilient relationships by fostering a communicative environment that values transparency and understanding.

Adding an element of flexibility and spontaneity to your interactions can also enhance the quality of your relationship. While routine and predictability are important, especially for children with ODD, occasional spontaneous activities can bring a refreshing change. They can be a fun way to break the monotony of daily life. This could be as simple as a surprise trip to get ice cream or an impromptu movie night. These surprises can bring joy and excitement, helping to relieve stress and build positive memories. They remind your child that beyond the routines and rules, there's a relationship full of love and fun.

Incorporating these elements of quality time—regularly scheduled activities, active participation, meaningful conversations, and spontaneous fun—into your parenting approach can significantly strengthen the bond between you and your child. It creates a nurturing environment that fosters trust and mutual respect, which are essential elements for any family but are especially critical in families navigating the challenges of ODD. Through these practices, you are not only addressing the immediate needs of your child but are also investing in a relationship that will support and enrich both of your lives for years to come.

5.4 ADDRESSING PARENTAL NEEDS AND RELATIONSHIP STRAINS

Parenting, particularly when faced with the challenges of a child with Oppositional Defiant Disorder, is a profoundly rewarding journey, yet it is not without its toll. Among the most critical aspects often overshadowed in the parenting discourse is the phenomenon of parental burnout—a state of emotional, mental, and frequently physical exhaustion caused by prolonged stress in parenting. It is characterized by fatigue, inefficacy, and emotional detachment from one's children. Recognizing the signs early—such as persistent tiredness, feeling overwhelmed or trapped, and diminishing joy in parenting and other areas of life—is essential. Early recognition provides a beacon for seeking necessary changes and implementing strategies to replenish your energy and well-being. Proactive steps might include setting aside time for self-care activities that rejuvenate your spirit, whether it's a hobby, exercise, meditation, or simply quiet time alone. Balancing the demands of parenting with personal well-being is not indulgent—it's indispensable for sustaining the long-term health and harmony of both parent and child.

Building a robust support system plays an invaluable role in navigating the complexities of raising a child with ODD. This network can include family members and friends, neighbors, and community resources such as parenting groups, online forums, and local organizations dedicated to behavioral disorders. These connections provide not only practical help and advice but also emotional support. Sharing your experiences with others who understand can significantly alleviate feelings of isolation and stress. For instance, joining a parent support group can offer a platform to exchange stories and strategies and sometimes just to vent in a safe, understanding environment. Community resources often provide workshops and seminars that can equip you with new tools and knowledge, empowering you to handle challenges more effectively. Engaging with these networks encourages a sense of community and mutual support, which is essential for maintaining emotional resilience.

In the whirlwind of parenting, especially under challenging circumstances, the relationship with your partner can sometimes take a backseat. However, maintaining a healthy, supportive relationship with your partner is crucial for your own well-being and as a model for your child's understanding of healthy adult relationships. Regularly dedicating time to spend together without the children is vital. This can be as simple as a date night, a regular evening walk, or a shared activity that both of you enjoy. These moments allow you to reconnect, communicate openly, and strengthen your partnership away from the immediate pressures of parenting. It's also a space where you can support each other's parenting efforts, discuss strategies, and make joint decisions, which can help prevent conflicts and discrepancies in handling the challenges posed by ODD.

There comes a point where the complexities of family dynamics or the intensity of the strains might require professional intervention. Seeking help from a family counselor or therapist can provide a constructive way to address issues that seem beyond your ability to manage alone. Therapy can offer new perspectives, coping strategies, and a structured approach to resolving conflicts and improving family dynamics. It's a proactive step towards healing and strengthening family relationships, particularly when the stress levels impact the family's overall functioning. Professional guidance can be especially beneficial in navigating the emotional complexities and helping each family member feel heard and supported. Engaging in family therapy is a testament to the commitment to the family's well-being. It can be a pivotal step in restoring balance and harmony.

Adopting these strategies not only supports your capacity as a parent but also safeguards the emotional climate of your home, making it a nurturing place for everyone. Recognizing your needs and addressing relationship strains are not just supplementary aspects of parenting; they are crucial for the health and success of your family unit. By taking care of your own emotional and relational health, you set the stage for a more positive, practical approach to parenting and a more joyful, cohesive family life.

5.5 CELEBRATING SMALL WINS WITH YOUR FAMILY

In the landscape of parenting a child with Oppositional Defiant Disorder (ODD), each day may present its set of challenges, often overshadowing the small, positive moments. Recognizing and celebrating these 'small wins' can dramatically shift the family atmosphere from constant stress to ongoing encouragement and joy. Teaching parents to identify these small successes is crucial.

These wins could be anything from a day with fewer outbursts, a moment of kindness, or even a task completed with less resistance than usual. For instance, your child managing to share a toy with a sibling or completing homework on time are achievements worth recognizing. Highlighting these moments can reinforce positive behaviors, showing your child that their efforts are noticed and valued, which can motivate them to continue their progress.

Creating a culture of recognition within the family involves regular, intentional actions celebrating each member's achievements. This practice fosters a positive family environment where everyone feels valued for their contributions, not just the children but also the parents. Implementing a weekly family celebration can be an effective way to do this. Perhaps every Sunday, each family member can share something they feel proud of from the past week, and the family can celebrate these accomplishments together. This ritual enhances family bonding and instills a sense of collective achievement and support. It's about building a family identity that thrives on mutual encouragement and appreciation.

Inclusivity in these celebrations is critical. Ensuring that every family member's achievements, no matter how small, are acknowledged and celebrated reinforces the idea that everyone's contributions are essential. This inclusivity is particularly vital in families with multiple children, where it's easy for one child's challenges or successes to overshadow another's. By celebrating all achievements equally, you help mitigate feelings of jealousy or competition among siblings and instead promote a supportive family dynamic. For example, while one child's improvement in handling frustration might be celebrated, another's success in a school project should be equally applauded. This balance helps maintain a harmonious and supportive home environment where each child feels equally important and valued.

Reflective Practices to Enhance Family Bonding

Integrating reflection and gratitude practices into your family life can further deepen bonds and enhance the overall emotional climate of your home. Regular family meetings that include a segment for reflecting on what went well during the week or expressing gratitude for each other's support can be compelling. During these meetings, encourage each family member to share something they are thankful for, whether it's help received from another family member, something they learned, or a simple moment of joy. These reflections foster a positive outlook and help develop a habit of looking for and appreciating the good in each day rather than focusing solely on challenges.

For instance, start a family gratitude jar where each member can drop notes about good things that happen each day and then read them together at the end of the week or month. This visual and interactive element can make the practice more engaging, especially for younger children, and serve as a powerful reminder of the family's many positive experiences and achievements. Moreover, it teaches children to recognize and articulate the good in their lives, which can counterbalance the frustrations and challenges they might face, especially for those with ODD.

By emphasizing the importance of recognizing and celebrating small wins within the family, fostering an inclusive culture of recognition, and incorporating reflective and gratitude practices, you enhance individual self-esteem and motivation and strengthen familial bonds. These practices create a supportive and positive family environment where each member feels valued and connected, paving the way for continued growth and harmony.

As we conclude this chapter, we reflect on the transformative power of celebrating small wins and fostering a positive family culture. The practices discussed here are not just strategies for managing a child with ODD but foundational elements for building a supportive and nurturing family environment. By recognizing and celebrating each family member's achievements, fostering inclusivity, and engaging in reflective practices, you create a family dynamic that supports and uplifts all members. These elements are crucial for navigating the challenges of ODD and enhancing the quality of family life.

The next chapter will explore holistic and alternative approaches to managing ODD, expanding our toolkit for supporting our children in more comprehensive and creative ways.

MAKE A DIFFERENCE WITH YOUR REVIEW

UNLOCK THE POWER OF GENEROSITY

"Money can't buy happiness, but giving it away can."

FREDDIE MERCURY

People who give without expecting anything in return live longer, happier lives and make more money. So, if we have a chance to do that during our time together, I'm definitely going to try.

To make that happen, I have a question for you...

Would you help someone you've never met, even if you never got credit for it?

Who is this person you ask? They are like you. Or, at least, like you used to be. Less experienced, wanting to make a difference, and needing help, but still trying to figure out where to look.

Our mission is to make [Oppositional Defiant Disorder Simplified] accessible to everyone. Everything I do stems from that mission. And, the only way for me to accomplish that mission is by reaching...well...everyone.

This is where you come in. Most people do, in fact, judge a book by its cover (and its reviews). So here's my ask on behalf of a struggling parent you've never met:

Please help that parent by leaving this book a review.

Your gift costs no money and takes less than 60 seconds to make real, but it can change a fellow parent's life forever. Your review could help…

…one more family find peace. …one more parent understands their child better. …one more child feels more supported. …one more family to improve their dynamics. …one more dream of a happy family that has come true.

To get that 'feel good' feeling and help this person for real, all you have to do is leave a review, and it takes less than 60 seconds.

Scan the QR code below to leave your review:

If you feel good about helping a faceless parent, you are my kind of person. Welcome to the club. You're one of us.

I'm even more excited to help you improve your family dynamics faster and easier than you can possibly imagine. You'll love the  practical tips and strategies I'll share in the coming chapters.

Thank you from the bottom of my heart. Now, back to our regularly scheduled program.

- Your biggest fan, Charlene Collins

PS - Fun fact: If you provide something of value to another person, it makes you more valuable to them. If you'd like goodwill straight from another parent - and believe this book will help them - send it their way.

CHAPTER 6
HOLISTIC AND ALTERNATIVE APPROACHES

Navigating the complexities of Oppositional Defiant Disorder (ODD) often requires more than traditional behavioral strategies and interventions. It invites an exploration into holistic approaches encompassing every aspect of lifestyle, from diet and nutrition to the environment surrounding the child. This chapter delves into how integrating holistic methods can provide a complementary framework to enhance children with ODD's well-being and behavioral responses. Here, you'll discover the significant role that diet and nutrition play in managing behavioral symptoms, offering practical, everyday solutions beyond the therapy room.

6.1 DIET, NUTRITION, AND ODD: WHAT PARENTS SHOULD KNOW

Understanding the Connection Between Diet and Behavior

The adage "you are what you eat" holds more truth than one might suspect, especially regarding behavioral health. Emerging research continues to shed light on the profound impact nutritional status has on behavioral outcomes, particularly in children with behavioral disorders such as ODD. Certain deficiencies in diet or specific food sensitivities can exacerbate symptoms associated with ODD, including irritability, aggression, and resistance to authority.

For instance, studies have indicated that a lack of essential nutrients like omega-3 fatty acids, zinc, and magnesium might contribute to difficulties in emotional regulation and impulse control—both critical challenges faced by children with ODD. Moreover, food additives and colorings, often abundant in processed foods, have been linked in some research to increased hyperactivity and lower concentration levels in susceptible children. Understanding these connections can empower you to make informed dietary choices that might mitigate some of these behavioral issues and enhance overall health.

Key Nutrients for Brain Health

Focusing on a diet rich in key nutrients can play a crucial role in managing ODD symptoms effectively. Omega-3 fatty acids, for instance, are essential for brain health, promoting better cognitive function and emotional regulation. Sources like salmon, sardines, flaxseeds, and walnuts are rich in these fatty acids. They can be a beneficial addition to your child's diet.

Zinc is another nutrient that's been shown to positively influence behavior. It plays a vital role in neurotransmitter function, which is crucial for maintaining calm and focus in children. Foods rich in zinc include beef, pumpkin seeds, and lentils. Similarly, magnesium, often called the calming mineral, helps nerve function and can reduce irritability and hyperactivity. Incorporating magnesium-rich foods like leafy greens, nuts, yogurt, and whole grains can help maintain a balanced mood.

Implementing a Balanced Diet

Transitioning to a balanced diet that supports optimal brain health involves more than just adding a few essential foods; it requires a holistic shift in how we approach eating. Start by gradually increasing the presence of whole foods in your child's diet while reducing the intake of processed foods, particularly those high in sugar and artificial additives.

Here's a simple, balanced meal plan for a day that incorporates these principles:

- Breakfast: Oatmeal topped with walnuts and slices of banana. Oats are high in fiber and magnesium, while bananas provide a natural sweetness and are rich in potassium, which supports healthy nerve function.
- Lunch: Grilled salmon with a side of steamed broccoli and quinoa. This meal combines Omega-3 fatty acids, protein, and fiber, all essential for brain health and stable energy levels throughout the day.
- Dinner: Stir-fried beef with bell peppers and brown rice. This meal contains zinc and other minerals essential for neurotransmitter function and overall brain health.

Snacks can include yogurt with fresh berries or slices of apple with almond butter, providing additional nutrients and energy between meals.

Considering Elimination Diets

For some children with ODD, elimination diets that cut out specific allergens like gluten or dairy or additives like artificial colors and preservatives may lead to an improvement in behavior. This approach should be considered carefully and implemented in a structured manner to ensure the child receives all necessary nutrients. Start by eliminating one food group at a time and observe any changes in behavior over a few weeks. This method helps pinpoint specific sensitivities and their impact on your child's behavior, allowing for a more tailored dietary approach that suits their needs.

Effectively monitoring these changes requires close observation and maintaining a food diary. In this diary, note what foods were consumed and any behavioral changes. This record can be valuable in understanding how diet affects your child's behavior and guiding future dietary choices.

By embracing these nutritional strategies, you embark on a path that enhances your child's dietary habits and mitigates the behavioral challenges associated with ODD. This holistic approach to diet and nutrition offers a complementary tool in your broader strategy to manage ODD, empowering you with actionable steps that contribute to a calmer, more stable home environment.

6.2 THE ROLE OF EXERCISE IN MANAGING ODD

Regular physical activity is not just important for physical health but also plays a crucial role in mental and emotional well-being, particularly for children with Oppositional Defiant Disorder (ODD). Consistent exercise can significantly improve mood, reduce anxiety, and enhance emotional regulation. This positive impact is primarily due to the release of endorphins, often known as 'feel-good' hormones, natural stress fighters our bodies produce. When your child engages in physical activity, their brain releases these hormones, which act as mood lifters and natural painkillers. This biochemical process can lead to noticeable improvements in their general disposition, making them feel more relaxed and less prone to outbursts or aggression.

Moreover, regular exercise helps regulate sleep patterns and improve concentration, which can be challenging for children with ODD. A good night's sleep after a day that includes physical activity can be deeper and more restful, which is crucial since sleep issues often exacerbate behavioral problems. Also, following a routine in sports can teach children the value of structure and lead to better focus and dedication in other areas of their lives, including academics and relationships.

Turning to specific activities that are particularly beneficial, team sports can be an excellent option for children with ODD as they offer opportunities to develop social skills, learn cooperation, and understand the importance of following rules. Soccer, basketball, or even doubles tennis require working with others towards a common goal, which can help curb tendencies of defiance against authority figures and peers. Meanwhile, martial arts are excellent for instilling discipline and self-control. They focus on physical strength, mental growth, respect for others, and self-discipline. The structured environment of martial arts classes teaches children about hierarchy, respect, and the consequences of their actions in a controlled setting.

Furthermore, practices like yoga can be exceptionally beneficial in enhancing calmness. Yoga combines physical postures with breathing exercises and meditation, helping children improve their body awareness and emotional regulation. It teaches them how to stay present and calm, which can be particularly beneficial for those with ODD who may struggle with impulsivity and agitation.

Incorporating regular physical activity into your child's routine should be done thoughtfully to ensure it is both enjoyable and sustainable. Start by choosing activities that align with your child's interests to increase motivation. If they love nature, consider hiking or organized outdoor games for a child fascinated by how things work. Swimming or gymnastics might be appealing due to the mechanics of the movements. It's also important to set realistic goals to avoid overwhelming them; starting with short sessions and gradually increasing the duration as they build stamina and interest is vital. Celebrate milestones to keep them motivated, such as mastering a new skill or improving their personal best in a sport, which can boost their confidence and encourage them to stay engaged.

Case Studies and Success Stories

Reflecting on the transformative impact of exercise, consider the story of Lucas, a 10-year-old boy diagnosed with ODD. Struggling with aggression and a short temper, Lucas found engaging positively with peers and adults complex. However, after joining a local soccer team, his behavior began to show remarkable improvement. The structured nature of the team activities helped him develop better social interactions, and the physical exercise helped moderate his mood swings. Another success story involves Ava, a 12-year-old with ODD who discovered yoga through a school program. Initially resistant to participate, she eventually found the breathing exercises and flowing movements a powerful outlet for her frustrations, significantly decreasing her daily outbursts.

These stories underscore the potential of physical activities to entertain, heal, and transform. Regular engagement in these activities can be a pivotal part of children with ODD's overall behavioral management strategy, providing them with tools to better manage their emotions and interact with the world around them.

6.3 MINDFULNESS PRACTICES FOR KIDS AND PARENTS

Introducing mindfulness into your family's routine can be transformative, especially when navigating the complexities of Oppositional Defiant Disorder (ODD). Mindfulness is about cultivating active, open attention to the present moment. When practiced regularly, it can significantly decrease reactivity and increase emotional regulation—both of which are often challenging for children with ODD. By learning to respond to situations with awareness rather than reacting impulsively, mindfulness helps manage stress. It reduces the frequency and intensity of emotional outbursts for you and your child.

For children, mindfulness techniques need to be engaging and easy to grasp. One effective method is guided breathing, which is taught using fun imagery. For instance, you can encourage your child to imagine blowing up a balloon with their breath, focusing on slow, deep breaths that expand their belly and chest. This helps center their thoughts and control their breathing, a powerful tool for calming the nervous system during moments of distress.

Another technique is listening to a bell. You can use a soft-toned bell and ask your child to listen carefully to the sound until it ultimately fades away. This exercise helps enhance focus and teaches children to concentrate on the present moment, reducing impulsivity. Mindful coloring, another popular activity, involves coloring sheets with intricate patterns that require attention to detail. This activity is therapeutic and keeps children engaged and quiet, helping them practice mindfulness while indulging in a creative pursuit.

Incorporating these mindfulness exercises into your daily routines can help make them a natural part of your child's life. Perhaps start a 'mindful minute' every morning before breakfast or introduce a 'breathing space' during homework time. This can help reset your child's focus and calm. It's about finding moments throughout the day that lend themselves to these practices and making mindfulness a regular, predictable part of your child's daily environment.

Parent-Child Mindfulness Practices

Mindfulness practices can strengthen your relationship with your child, providing a shared toolset for managing emotions and stress. One simple yet powerful practice is the 'heart-to-heart' breathing exercise. Sit face to face with your child, your knees almost touching, and hold hands. Guide your child to breathe in sync with you, slowly and deeply. This helps calm down and synchronizes your emotional states, enhancing empathy and connection. Another effective practice is the 'body scan' technique, where you and your child can lie on the floor side by side and slowly bring attention to different body parts. This practice promotes relaxation and enhances bodily awareness, which is often needed for children who experience intense emotions.

These shared activities not only provide immediate calming effects but also teach your child valuable self-regulation skills that they can apply independently over time. By practicing together, you guide them in learning these techniques and show your commitment to the practice, which can be highly motivating for them.

Resources for Learning and Practicing Mindfulness

Numerous resources are available to further support your mindfulness journey, guiding you and your child through various practices. Apps like 'Headspace' and 'Calm' offer guided meditations and mindfulness exercises specifically designed for children, making the practice accessible and engaging. These digital platforms provide a range of activities that can be easily integrated into daily routines, from short, animated meditations to bedtime stories that incorporate mindfulness themes.

Books can also be an excellent resource. For younger children, 'Sitting Still Like a Frog' by Eline Snel contains mindfulness exercises tailored to children that help with emotion regulation, concentration, and stress management. For older children and teenagers, 'The Mindful Teen' by Dzung X. Vo offers practical advice and mindfulness practices designed to help teens deal with their daily challenges. These books provide techniques and deeper insights into how mindfulness can be a transformative tool for emotional and mental well-being.

By integrating these mindfulness practices into your family's life, you're not just helping manage the symptoms of ODD but also fostering an environment of calm and focus that benefits all aspects of life. Whether through simple breathing exercises, shared mindfulness sessions, or digital and print resources, the tools you integrate into your daily routine can profoundly impact your child's ability to navigate the challenges of ODD with greater calm and resilience.

6.4 THE IMPACT OF ART AND MUSIC THERAPY

Art and music therapy represent transformative approaches beyond traditional behavioral management techniques, offering unique emotional expression and regulation pathways. These therapies provide essential outlets for children who might struggle to articulate their complex feelings verbally, allowing them to explore and process their emotions through creative expression. This can be particularly beneficial for children with Oppositional Defiant Disorder (ODD), who often experience intense emotions and may not yet have the skills to express them constructively.

The therapeutic benefits of art and music are well-documented, with studies showing significant improvements in emotional and behavioral responses among children who engage in these activities. Art therapy, for instance, involves using materials like paints, clay, or markers to create artwork as a form of emotional release. Creating art can be a safe and controlled space for children to express anger, frustration, or sadness without words. Making art can also help children visualize their emotions and gain insights into their feelings, which can be a decisive step toward understanding and managing their behaviors.

Similarly, music therapy offers a dynamic way to assist children in processing emotions and reducing stress. Whether it's through playing instruments, singing, or even just listening to certain types of music, music's rhythmic and melodic elements can facilitate a calming effect on the brain and body. For a child with ODD, engaging in music therapy can be a way to redirect negative behaviors and channel energy into a productive and soothing activity. Music has the unique ability to match or alter our moods, and choosing music that mirrors a child's feelings can validate their emotions, while slowly shifting to more calming or uplifting music can guide them to a more positive emotional state.

Implementing Art Therapy at Home

Introducing art therapy at home does not require extensive art supplies or any previous artistic skill, both on your part and your child's. It starts with creating a safe, welcoming space where your child feels free to express themselves without judgment. This could be a dedicated room corner with easy access to art supplies. Please encourage your child to draw, paint, or model with clay, whatever comes to their mind, especially when they feel overwhelmed or upset. Simple activities like coloring mandalas or free drawing can significantly help focus a child's mind and calm their emotions.

Explaining to your child how these activities can help them might increase their willingness to participate. For instance, you might say, "Sometimes, when we're feeling really mad or sad, it helps to make something with our hands. Let's see if drawing how you feel right now might make things easier." This approach sets the stage for emotional processing. It enhances your child's coping skills, providing them with tools they can use independently over time.

Role of Music Therapy in Emotional Expression and Regulation

To incorporate music therapy into your child's routine, observe the types of music they are naturally drawn to. Create a playlist of songs they enjoy and another that includes calming, instrumental tracks. Encourage your child to listen to music when they feel the onset of frustration or anger, and use headphones if that helps them tune out distractions. Additionally, learning to play a simple instrument like a keyboard, drum, or even a ukulele can provide a constructive focus for your child's energy and emotions.

Playing music requires concentration and physical interaction, which can be great for children needing to regulate their emotions. It's also a skill-building activity that boosts their self-esteem and provides a sense of accomplishment. For emotional regulation, rhythm plays a crucial role. Engaging your child in rhythm exercises, such as clapping to a beat or playing a rhythm on a drum, can help synchronize their body's responses to their emotions, leading to greater emotional control.

Finding Professional Art and Music Therapists

While implementing art and music therapy at home can be beneficial, working with a professional therapist can deepen the therapeutic effects. Professional art and music therapists are trained to guide children through the creative process in ways that specifically aim to address emotional and behavioral issues. To find a qualified therapist, consult your child's pediatrician or a mental health professional who can provide referrals. Additionally, reputable organizations such as the American Art Therapy Association and the American Music Therapy Association offer directories of certified therapists.

When choosing a therapist, it's essential to look for individuals who have experience working with children, especially those with behavioral disorders like ODD. During initial sessions, observe how the therapist interacts with your child and ensure that their approach aligns with your child's needs and personality. A good therapist will not only engage your child in therapeutic activities but also teach them skills they can continue using outside of therapy sessions.

By exploring the world of art and music therapy, you provide your child with innovative tools for expression and coping that enrich their emotional landscape and offer new pathways for personal growth and behavioral management. These therapies, whether practiced at home or with a professional, can significantly enhance your child's ability to express and regulate their emotions, contributing to a more harmonious family environment and a fuller, more expressive life for your child.

6.5 HOMEOPATHY AND HERBAL SUPPLEMENTS: WHAT PARENTS SHOULD KNOW

In exploring the spectrum of holistic and alternative approaches to managing Oppositional Defiant Disorder (ODD), it's valuable to consider the role of homeopathy and herbal supplements. These treatments stem from philosophical and practical foundations different from conventional medicine and offer unique perspectives on health and wellness. Homeopathy, for instance, is based on the principle of "like cures like," suggesting that substances capable of causing disease symptoms in healthy individuals can, when administered in highly diluted amounts, treat similar symptoms in sick individuals. Herbal supplements, on the other hand, use various parts of plants—leaves, roots, berries, and flowers—for medicinal purposes, aiming to harness the natural chemical properties of these plants to support health and treat illnesses.

For parents navigating the complexities of ODD, understanding how these approaches might benefit their child can provide additional tools for managing the disorder. Some proponents of homeopathy and herbalism argue that specific remedies can help alleviate symptoms commonly associated with ODD, such as irritability, quick temper, and defiance. For example, the homeopathic remedy Chamomilla is often recommended for children who exhibit irritability and restlessness, while Valerian root, a widely used herbal supplement, is known for its calming effects and might be considered to help manage aggressive behaviors and promote better sleep.

However, it's crucial to approach these treatments carefully, particularly regarding their integration with other management strategies your child might be following. Consulting with health-care professionals familiar with conventional and alternative medicine can provide guidance tailored to your child's specific needs, ensuring that any treatment plan, including homeopathy or herbal supplements, is safe and effective. This consultation is vital as it helps prevent potential interactions between different therapies and ensures that the chosen remedies complement rather than contradict other treatments.

Reviewing Scientific Evidence

While anecdotal evidence supports the benefits of homeopathy and herbal supplements for various conditions, the scientific community remains divided regarding their efficacy, especially in treating behavioral disorders like ODD. Research in these areas often faces methodological challenges, such as small sample sizes and lack of placebo control, which can affect the reliability of the results. For instance, studies on the effectiveness of St. John's Wort for treating mild depression have shown promising results; however, its impact on behavioral disorders is less clear, with more rigorous research needed to draw definitive conclusions.

Given this context, it's essential to critically review the available evidence and consider these treatments as potential complements to more conventional therapies rather than replacements. Engaging with professionals in pediatric behavioral health and alternative medicine can provide insights into the most current and relevant research, helping you make informed decisions about incorporating these treatments into your child's care plan.

As you consider the potential of homeopathy and herbal supplements to support your child's journey with ODD, remember that every child responds differently to various treatments. What works for one child might not be effective for another, even if they share similar symptoms. Therefore, monitoring your child's response to any new treatment is crucial. Keeping a detailed record of their behaviors and any changes observed with the introduction of new remedies can help you and your healthcare provider determine the effectiveness of the treatment and make necessary adjustments.

This exploration into homeopathy and herbal supplements highlights the broader landscape of holistic approaches you might consider for managing ODD. As with any aspect of healthcare, especially when it involves young children with behavioral challenges, informed, cautious, and personalized approaches are critical. By understanding the potential benefits and the limitations of these alternative treatments, you can better navigate the options available and choose those that best fit your child's needs and your family's values.

As we conclude this chapter on holistic and alternative approaches, we reflect on the diverse options for managing ODD. From nutritional adjustments and physical activities to mindfulness practices and the thoughtful use of homeopathy and herbal supplements, each element offers unique benefits that can complement traditional therapies. As you integrate these strategies, the overarching goal remains to comprehensively support your child's health and well-being, paving the way for more effective management of ODD and a balanced, harmonious family life.

CHAPTER 7
THERAPEUTIC INTERVENTIONS AND SUPPORTS

Navigating the complexities of Oppositional Defiant Disorder (ODD) can sometimes feel like attempting to navigate a maze where the walls keep shifting. It's a journey that requires patience, understanding, and the right strategies. This chapter delves into the therapeutic interventions that can make a significant difference in your child's life and your family dynamics. Cognitive Behavioral Therapy (CBT) stands out as a convenient approach for children with ODD. Let's explore how this therapy works, the techniques it employs, and how you, as a parent, can be actively involved in this transformative process.

7.1 COGNITIVE BEHAVIORAL THERAPY: A GUIDE FOR PARENTS

Introduction to Cognitive Behavioral Therapy (CBT)

Cognitive Behavioral Therapy (CBT) is a form of psychological treatment that has been consistently found effective in various disorders such as anxiety and depression, and, notably, Oppositional Defiant Disorder (ODD). The core principle of CBT is relatively straightforward yet profound: our thoughts and perceptions influence our behaviors and emotions. In the context of ODD, this therapy helps children understand and modify the thought patterns that lead to defiant behavior, enabling them to respond to challenging situations more positively.

CBT is structured, goal-oriented, and focuses on the immediate problems. It empowers children by teaching them that while they cannot control every aspect of the world around them, they can control how they interpret and deal with things in their environment. For a child with ODD, who may often feel that situations or demands are hostile or unfair, CBT offers a toolkit for reevaluating their perceptions and responding in a way that is less about opposition and more about constructive responses.

CBT Techniques for ODD

CBT for ODD involves specific strategies tailored to address the unique challenges associated with the disorder. One of the primary techniques is cognitive restructuring, which helps children identify and challenge the often negative automatic thoughts that can lead to disruptive behavior. For example, if a child thinks, "My teacher always picks on me," CBT works to transform that thought into something more balanced, like, "My teacher enforces rules with everyone in class, not just me." This shift can reduce feelings of defensiveness and promote more adaptive behavior in the classroom.

Behavioral experiments are another crucial aspect of CBT. These controlled scenarios encourage children to test the accuracy of their negative beliefs and assumptions in a safe setting. For instance, a child who believes that "no one likes me" might be encouraged to initiate a conversation with a peer. The positive outcome of such an experiment can challenge and gradually change the child's fundamental beliefs about their social interactions.

Emotion regulation training is also integral. Children with ODD often experience intense emotions and have difficulty managing them. CBT provides them practical skills to calm themselves when upset, such as deep breathing, counting to ten, or stepping away from a stressful situation. These techniques help them to pause and choose a more thoughtful response instead of reacting impulsively.

Role of Parents in CBT

Parents play a crucial role in their child's success with CBT. Your involvement can range from participating in therapy sessions to reinforcing the concepts at home. Therapists often provide specific strategies parents can use to complement the therapy sessions. For example, you might be taught how to provide effective feedback, reinforce positive behavior, and maintain consistency in expectations and consequences.

At home, you can help by creating an environment that supports the CBT principles. This might involve setting up scenarios that allow your child to practice their new skills or ensuring that you model positive cognitive and behavioral responses yourself. Your support in applying CBT techniques consistently at home is vital in helping your child generalize these new skills to various settings.

Finding a Qualified CBT Practitioner

Selecting the right therapist is crucial to the effectiveness of CBT. When looking for a CBT practitioner, it's essential to find someone who is qualified and experienced in working with children, particularly those with ODD. Credentials to look for include certification in cognitive behavioral therapy and a background in pediatric psychology or psychiatry.

When meeting potential therapists, ask about their ODD experience, approach to involving parents in therapy, and examples of success stories. It's also helpful to understand their methodology for assessing progress. A good therapist will welcome these questions and be transparent about their methods and outcomes.

Interactive Element: Questions to Consider When Choosing a CBT Therapist

- What is your experience with treating children who have Oppositional Defiant Disorder?
- How do you involve parents in the therapy process?
- Can you share any success stories or case studies?
- How do you measure progress in therapy?

Selecting the appropriate therapist is an essential step in effectively managing your child's ODD through CBT. It ensures that the therapy provided meets your child's specific needs and aligns with your family's goals for growth and harmony.

In sum, Cognitive Behavioral Therapy offers robust tools and strategies for managing ODD, focusing on changing the thought patterns that lead to defiant behavior. Understanding and implementing CBT and choosing the right therapist can provide your child with valuable skills that promote better behavior and emotional responses, significantly enhancing family dynamics and your child's ability to navigate their world. As we continue exploring other therapeutic interventions and supports in this chapter, keep in mind the central role of informed, proactive parental involvement in the success of any therapeutic approach.

7.2 UNDERSTANDING THE ROLE OF MEDICATION

Medication can be a sensitive topic when it comes to managing behavioral issues in children, particularly for those diagnosed with Oppositional Defiant Disorder (ODD). While not a first-line treatment, medication may be considered in specific instances where a child's symptoms are severe and have not responded to other interventions or when they co-occur with other disorders such as ADHD or anxiety. These scenarios often present a complex challenge where the interplay between different symptoms may exacerbate the child's overall condition, affecting their ability to benefit from therapeutic interventions alone.

For instance, a child with ODD who also suffers from significant anxiety might find it extremely difficult to engage in cognitive-physical symptoms of anxiety, which could overpower their ability to process and utilize the coping strategies being taught. In such cases, medication might be prescribed to manage the stress, thereby lowering the barrier to effective participation in therapy. Similarly, suppose a child's impulsive and hyperactive behaviors associated with ADHD exacerbate their defiance and opposition. In that case, medication might help manage these ADHD symptoms, indirectly reducing the ODD symptoms by enabling the child to engage more effectively with behavioral strategies.

When discussing medication for ODD, it is essential to consider the most commonly prescribed types that target co-occurring conditions, as there are no medications specifically approved to treat ODD alone. For ADHD symptoms, stimulant medications like methylphenidate (Ritalin) or amphetamines (Adderall) are commonly used and can reduce impulsivity and hyperactivity. For anxiety, selective serotonin reuptake inhibitors (SSRIs) like fluoxetine (Prozac) or sertraline (Zoloft) are often prescribed. These medications can help manage the anxiety symptoms, making it easier for the child to engage with life's daily demands more calmly.

Each medication has potential side effects, which must be weighed against the benefits. Stimulants, while effective in managing ADHD, can sometimes lead to decreased appetite, difficulty sleeping, or increased anxiety, all of which need to be monitored closely. SSRIs, on the other hand, may cause side effects such as gastrointestinal upset, fatigue, or agitation. The decision to use medication should always involve:

- A detailed discussion with a healthcare provider.
- Focusing on a comprehensive evaluation of the child's behavioral patterns.
- Emotional needs.
- The overall family dynamics.

Making Informed Decisions About Medication

Choosing to use medication as part of your child's treatment plan is a significant decision and should be approached with thorough consideration and understanding. Having an open line of communication with your child's healthcare provider is essential. Here are some critical questions you might consider asking:

- What are the expected benefits of the medication for my child's specific symptoms?

- What are the potential side effects, and how can they be managed?
- How will the medication's effectiveness be monitored and evaluated?
- Are there any long-term implications of using this medication?

Discussing how the medication fits into the broader treatment plan is also crucial. Medication should not be viewed as a stand-alone solution but as one component of a comprehensive approach that includes behavioral therapies, educational interventions, and family support. This integrated approach ensures that all aspects of the child's well-being are addressed, enhancing the overall effectiveness of the treatment and promoting long-term positive outcomes.

Integrating medication with other treatments requires careful coordination. Regular follow-ups with the healthcare provider are essential to monitor the child's response to the medication and adjust the treatment plan as necessary. Communication with your child's school and therapists is crucial to ensure they know the medication. It can provide insights into how it might affect the child's behavior and engagement in different settings.

In summary, understanding when and how medication can be used effectively is crucial for parents managing a child with ODD, especially when other disorders are also present. Through careful consideration, informed discussions with healthcare providers, and integration into a broader treatment strategy, medication can play a vital role in helping your child achieve better emotional regulation and behavioral control. This approach addresses the immediate challenges and lays a foundation for long-term success and well-being.

7.3 THE IMPORTANCE OF SCHOOL-BASED INTERVENTIONS

Navigating the educational landscape for a child with Oppositional Defiant Disorder (ODD) requires a proactive approach and collaboration that extends beyond the home and into the school environment. Understanding and utilizing school-based interventions can significantly enhance your child's academic and social success. Practical cooperation with school personnel such as teachers, school counselors, and exceptional education staff is beneficial and essential. These professionals interact with your child in different settings and can provide valuable insights into their social interactions, learning styles, and responses to various teaching strategies.

Engaging actively with your child's school involves regular communication and meeting participation. It's essential to establish a relationship characterized by mutual respect and a common goal: the well-being and development of your child. Sharing your insights about your child's needs and behaviors can help educators create a more supportive learning environment. Additionally, being open to suggestions from teachers and other school staff can provide new strategies for managing behaviors that may be effective at school and home. This two-way exchange of information creates a partnership essential for consistently applying effective strategies across both environments.

Developing Individualized Education Programs (IEP) or 504 Plans is another critical component of school-based interventions for children with ODD. These plans are designed to provide accommodations supporting the child's educational needs. An IEP, available to children who qualify for special education, includes specific academic goals, tailored instructional strategies, and the necessary accommodations and services. For instance, if your child with ODD struggles with transitions between activities, an IEP might include a provision for advance warnings and assistance during changes in the school schedule.

A 504 Plan does not necessarily imply special education. Still, it provides accommodations that ensure a child has access to the same education as their peers. For example, a child who experiences significant anxiety in large groups may be allowed to present a project to only the teacher or have the option to do it via video. Determining eligibility for these plans involves assessments and evaluations by educational professionals, and as a parent, your involvement and advocacy play pivotal roles in this process.

Creating a Behavioral Intervention Plan (BIP)

A Behavioral Intervention Plan (BIP) can be a crucial part of an IEP or 504 Plan, specifically tailored to address behavioral challenges in the educational setting. A BIP is developed through a systematic process that includes observing the child, identifying triggers for undesirable behaviors, and determining the best strategies to alter or manage these behaviors. For example, suppose a child tends to act out during group activities. In that case, the BIP might include strategies like providing a clear outline of expected behavior before the activity or assigning a role that keeps the child actively engaged, thus reducing disruptive behavior.

The effectiveness of a BIP depends on consistent application and regular monitoring. It requires a collaborative effort among all school personnel who interact with the child, ensuring that everyone responds to behaviors in a way that reinforces the desired outcomes. Regular reviews of the BIP are necessary to assess its effectiveness and make adjustments based on the child's progress and evolving needs.

Advocating for Your Child's Needs

Advocating for your child within the school system can sometimes feel daunting. Preparation is key. Before meetings, gather observations and any documentation related to your child's behavior and progress. Know what accommodations have been adequate and what areas need additional support. Understanding your child's legal rights under education law can empower you to advocate more effectively. This might include familiarizing yourself with the Individuals with Disabilities Education Act (IDEA) or Section 504 of the Rehabilitation Act, which are federal laws that provide protections for students with disabilities.

Clear, respectful communication is vital when advocating for your child. Express appreciation for the educators' efforts and emphasize your desire to work collaboratively. If disagreements arise, focus on your child's needs rather than personal differences. Sometimes, bringing an advocate or a mental health professional who understands your child's needs can help articulate concerns and suggest appropriate accommodations.

In summary, school-based interventions play a critical role in supporting a child with ODD. Understanding the available educational accommodations and collaborating with school personnel can create a supportive environment that facilitates your child's success. Whether through regular communication with teachers, involvement in developing IEPs and BIPs, or effective advocacy, your proactive involvement is crucial to harnessing the educational system's resources to support your child's academic journey.

7.4 NAVIGATING INSURANCE AND ACCESS TO THERAPIES

Understanding the intricacies of insurance coverage for mental health services can be as complex as managing the symptoms of Oppositional Defiant Disorder (ODD) itself. When you begin the process, you might find that obtaining the necessary support for your child involves navigating a labyrinth of policy details, coverage limits, and eligibility criteria. Typically, private health insurance plans will cover a range of mental health services. Still, the extent of this coverage can vary significantly. It's crucial to start by thoroughly reviewing your insurance policy. Pay particular attention to sections on mental health and behavioral therapy coverage. Look for details about co-pays, deductibles, caps on the number of sessions per year, and whether or not you need a referral from a primary care provider to see a specialist. It's often helpful to contact your insurance provider directly to ask specific questions about what treatments are covered, especially those relevant to ODD, and to confirm whether the therapists or specialists you are considering are within your provider network.

Navigating insurance can sometimes lead to denials of coverage for specific therapies crucial for managing ODD. These denials can be based on the insurance company's assessment of the treatment as being "not medically necessary" or "experimental." If you face such a denial, it is essential to appeal the decision. Most insurance plans offer a process for appeal, and exercising this right can sometimes reverse the decision. Prepare for your appeal by gathering detailed documentation from your child's healthcare providers about the necessity of the therapy and its relevance to treating ODD. Submitting a well-prepared appeal that includes letters from your child's therapists, detailed treatment plans, and scientific articles about the effectiveness of the proposed therapy can increase your chances of a successful outcome.

For many families, accessing necessary therapy and support goes beyond what insurance covers. Community resources can play a crucial role in filling these gaps. Community mental health centers often offer therapy and counseling services on a sliding scale based on income, making them a valuable resource for families needing affordable options. Additionally, non-profit organizations may offer grants or free services for children with specific disorders like ODD. Universities with psychology or psychiatry programs often have clinics that provide low-cost treatment options over-seen by qualified professionals. These clinics offer therapy and are usually at the forefront of the latest research and treatment methodologies, providing cutting-edge care at a reduced cost.

Persistence in seeking and securing the necessary support for your child is paramount. The landscape of insurance and healthcare services is often fraught with delays, denials, and bureaucratic hurdles. It can be discouraging sometimes, but maintaining your resolve and advocating for your child's needs is crucial. Keep detailed records of all your interactions with insurance companies and healthcare providers. Follow up regularly on pending claims or appeals, and don't hesitate to escalate issues when necessary. Remember, you are the most important advocate your child has. Your persistence will often make the difference in ensuring they receive the care they need.

In navigating these pathways, whether through insurance, community resources, or direct appeals, the goal remains clear: to secure the best possible support to manage and treat your child's ODD effectively. By understanding your insurance plan, preparing for potential challenges in coverage, leveraging community resources, and persisting in your advocacy, you can pave a way forward that supports your child's health and well-being in the most comprehensive manner possible.

7.5 HOW SUPPORT GROUPS CAN HELP YOUR FAMILY

Navigating the complexities of parenting a child with Oppositional Defiant Disorder (ODD) can often feel isolating. It's a path filled with unique challenges and situations that might seem incomprehensible to those who have yet to experience them first-hand. This is where support groups can become an invaluable resource for you and your family. Engaging with a community of parents who share similar experiences can provide comfort and practical advice and strategies that have been effective in similar situations. These groups offer a platform for emotional support, shared knowledge, and the understanding that you are not alone in this experience.

The benefits of joining a support group extend beyond the emotional relief of sharing your story with empathetic listeners. Such groups often become a treasure trove of coping strategies and behavioral management techniques. For instance, you might learn about a new approach to handling defiance or a recommendation for a specialist who has improved similar cases. Additionally, these meetings can sometimes host professionals who provide insights into therapeutic options and new research, further enriching your understanding and resources.

Finding the right support group is critical to gaining these benefits. Start by contacting local mental health organizations, which often have lists of support groups divided by topics or disorders. These organizations can direct you to groups specifically for parents of children with ODD. Online platforms can be invaluable if locality is a barrier or flexibility is a priority. Websites and social media groups offer forums and virtual meetings that can connect you with support at any time, from anywhere, breaking the limitations imposed by geography.

However, the choice between online and in-person groups depends on your preference and what you hope to gain from the interactions. In-person groups offer a tangible sense of community. In contrast, face-to-face meetings can foster deeper personal connections and a different level of emotional support. Conversely, online groups provide accessibility and anonymity, which can be comforting for those initially hesitant to share their experiences openly. Each format has its own set of advantages and challenges, and sometimes, participating in both types of groups can maximize the support and resources available to you.

If you find that there isn't a group that meets your needs, or if you are looking for a more tailored support network, consider starting your own. Initiating a support group can seem daunting, but with a few structured steps, it can create a highly supportive community. Begin by defining the focus of the group—ensure it addresses the specific needs of parents dealing with children diagnosed with ODD. Next, decide on the logistics; where and how often the meetings will be held, whether online or in-person. Recruiting members is next: you can reach out through community centers, schools, and online forums dedicated to mental health and parenting. Finally, setting clear goals for the group's goals in each meeting can help maintain focus and provide consistent value to all members.

Support groups serve not just as a means to share your journey but also as a platform to learn and grow together with others who understand the intricacies of raising a child with ODD. They reinforce the idea that the challenges are significant but not insurmountable when faced together. As you continue to navigate the often turbulent waters of parenting a child with ODD, remember that these communities offer not just a lifeline but a place of growth and learning.

The next chapter will transition from understanding the role of support groups to exploring maintaining personal well-being. It's crucial to realize that caring effectively for your child involves caring for yourself, too. We will delve into strategies for self-care that ensure you remain strong, resilient, and well-equipped to handle the demands of parenting a child with special needs.

CHAPTER 8

PARENTAL SELF-CARE AND STRESS MANAGEMENT

In the relentless hustle of parenting, especially when navigating the complex waves of Oppositional Defiant Disorder (ODD), it's easy for your own needs to slip quietly into the background. Yet, carving out time for self-care is not a luxury—it is essential to sustaining your ability to be the supportive, effective parent your child needs. Think of it as securing your own oxygen mask before assisting others; maintaining your well-being directly impacts your capacity to manage the challenges of parenting a child with ODD. This chapter guides you through practical, achievable self-care strategies that fit into your busy life, ensuring you preserve and enhance your health and happiness.

8.1 SIMPLE SELF-CARE PRACTICES FOR BUSY PARENTS

Integrate Quick Mindfulness Exercises

Amid a chaotic day, finding a moment for peace can seem impossible. However, mindfulness exercises can be a sanctuary of calm in the eye of the storm, and they don't require extensive time commitments. Simple practices like mindful breathing focused listening, or mindful walking can be integrated into your day in brief moments between activities. For instance, practice taking three deep, conscious breaths each time you transition from one task to another, or engage in focused listening for a minute, paying close attention to the sounds around you, whether it's the hum of the refrigerator or birds chirping outside. These practices help center your thoughts and reduce stress, quickly resetting your mental state.

Establish a Routine for Self-Care

Just as routines benefit your child, establishing a routine for your self-care activities can enhance your mental and physical well-being. Identify small pockets of time in your day that can be dedicated to self-care. This might be early in the morning before the rest of the house wakes up, during a midday break, or in the evening when things quiet down. Consistency is critical—spending 15 minutes reading a book, taking a brisk walk, or engaging in a hobby like gardening or painting. Make these activities a regular, non-negotiable part of your schedule, just as critical as any parenting responsibilities.

Utilize Technology for Relaxation

Technology can be a significant ally in your self-care regimen in our digital age. Numerous apps offer guided meditations, soothing music, or yoga sessions that you can access right from your home. Apps like Calm or Headspace provide structured mindfulness and meditation exercises that can be done in short intervals, ideal for busy parents. Similarly, YouTube hosts various yoga sessions ranging from 5-minute stretches to full-hour classes, allowing you to choose one that fits your schedule and comfort level. These resources make it easier to incorporate relaxation practices into your day, helping to alleviate stress without requiring you to spend time traveling to a class.

Embrace the Power of No

One of the most powerful tools in your self-care arsenal is learning to say no. As a parent, especially one dealing with the extra challenges of ODD, you're often pulled in multiple directions, with demands coming from family, work, schools, and social commitments. Evaluating these demands and recognizing when they detract from your well-being is crucial. Saying no to additional responsibilities or social engagements that cause stress doesn't make you a bad parent or friend; it makes you a wise one who knows your limits. Setting these boundaries protects your energy and well-being, ensuring you have the reserves to manage your child's needs effectively.

These self-care strategies are not just about improving your quality of life; they're about enhancing your capacity to be the calm, grounded, and present parent that your child with ODD needs. By taking care of yourself, you're also taking care of your family, ensuring you have the strength, patience, and clarity to navigate parenting challenges with love and effectiveness. As we move forward in this chapter, we will explore further techniques to manage stress effectively, making self-care a fundamental aspect of your parenting journey.

8.2 STRESS MANAGEMENT TECHNIQUES THAT PROMOTE WELLBEING

Teach Progressive Muscle Relaxation

When the day's tension builds up, not just in your mind but physically within your body, progressive muscle relaxation (PMR) can be an invaluable tool to reclaim a sense of calm. This technique involves tensing each muscle group in your body one at a time and then relaxing them, fostering physical relief and mental tranquility. To practice PMR:

1. Find a quiet spot where you can sit or lie down without interruptions.
2. Starting with your feet, tense the muscles as hard as you can for about five seconds, then release suddenly, feeling the tension flow away.
3. Move up through your body, from your legs to your stomach, hands, arms, shoulders, neck, and face, following the same tense-and-release pattern. This method can be particularly effective before bedtime, helping to alleviate any physical discomfort or restlessness that might hinder sleep.

By incorporating PMR into your nightly routine, you can enhance the quality of your sleep and your ability to handle stress more effectively during the day.

Promote Physical Activity

Regular physical exercise can act as a robust counterbalance to stress. Activities like walking, cycling, or participating in team sports improve physical health and boost mental well-being by releasing endorphins, the body's natural stress relievers. Choosing activities you genuinely enjoy is the key to maintaining a regular exercise regimen. If you love nature, consider hiking or jogging through local parks. If rhythm moves you, perhaps a dance class or Zumba might be enjoyable. Even everyday activities like gardening or brisk walking can significantly elevate your mood and reduce stress. Setting realistic goals, such as a daily 30-minute walk or a thrice-weekly workout session, can make regular physical activity more attainable. Remember that the aim is to find joy in physical activity, turning exercise from a task into a valued part of your routine and making it a sustainable and effective stress management strategy.

Introduce Journaling for Emotional Release

Journaling your thoughts and feelings can be a therapeutic method for managing the complexities of daily life, particularly when parenting a child with ODD. Keeping a journal allows you to express emotions like frustration, anxiety, or joy privately, unfiltered, providing a safe outlet for emotional release. Start by setting aside a few minutes daily to jot down your thoughts. This doesn't need to be a structured activity; instead, let it be a free-flowing expression of whatever comes to mind. This practice can help clarify your thoughts, identify patterns in your emotions or behaviors, and reflect on the joys and challenges of parenting. Over time, journaling can become a reflective practice that helps you process emotions and enhances self-awareness and personal growth, making it easier to manage stress and interact more positively with your family.

Advocate for Adequate Sleep

The impact of sleep on physical and mental health cannot be overstated—it rejuvenates the body, consolidates memories, and regulates mood. Yet, for many parents, especially those managing the added stress of ODD, getting enough quality sleep can be a challenge. To improve your sleep hygiene:

1. Make an effort to keep a consistent sleep schedule by going to bed and waking up at the same time each day, including weekends.
2. Create a restful environment in your bedroom, which might mean investing in comfortable bedding, using blackout curtains to block out light, or employing white noise machines to drown out background noise.
3. Avoid stimulants like caffeine and screen time at least an hour before bed, as they can interfere with your ability to fall asleep.

By prioritizing good sleep hygiene, you're not just improving your night's rest—you're enhancing your resilience and capacity to manage the day-to-day challenges of parenting a child with ODD.

8.3 BUILDING A SUPPORT NETWORK: FINDING COMMUNITY

Navigating the parenting path of a child with Oppositional Defiant Disorder (ODD) can often feel like a solitary journey. However, the power of community in this journey cannot be overstated. Engaging with others who understand firsthand the complexities you face can provide solace and practical strategies to improve your parenting experience. Online support groups have emerged as a vital resource for parents like you, offering a platform where you can connect with others across the globe at any time. These virtual communities allow you to share experiences, exchange resources, and support one another in real time, breaking down the physical barriers that often limit support access. Platforms such as Facebook groups, dedicated forums, and even WhatsApp groups focused on parenting children with behavioral challenges can be invaluable. The key benefit is the continuous availability of support; whether you're facing a challenging night or need advice on handling a specific incident, these groups provide immediate access to a community that understands and empathizes with your situation.

Moreover, engaging with these online forums can significantly expand your toolkit for managing ODD. Parents and professionals in these groups often share articles, conduct webinars, and discuss evidence-based practices you might not encounter in your local environment. This exchange of information can be particularly empowering, equipping you with knowledge and techniques that are both innovative and practical. However, while online groups offer remarkable support, face-to-face interaction remains significant. Local support groups facilitated by hospitals, community centers, or mental health organizations provide a different connection layer. These groups allow you to meet other parents in your community, share experiences, and support each other more personally and directly. The tangible presence of others facing similar challenges can foster a sense of belonging and mutual support that virtual interactions may not fully replicate.

These local groups often host guest speakers, including psychologists, educators, and therapists, who can provide professional insights and guidance. Participating in these meetings helps you feel less isolated and offers practical, localized resources that can be immediately applicable in your day-to-day life. For instance, learning about local therapeutic services or educational accommodations available in your district can significantly affect how you manage your child's needs. Beyond structured support groups, the informal networks you create in your daily interactions at school events, playgrounds, or sports activities are equally beneficial. These casual acquaintances can grow into friendships where you find empathy, joy, and relaxation. Organizing playdates, sharing responsibilities for school pickups, or simply having a friend who understands your day-to-day challenges can lighten your emotional load.

Friendships with other parents provide a safe space to share frustrations and successes without judgment, making your social outings an essential outlet for stress relief. Lastly, consider the benefits of respite care services while building your support network. Parenting a child with ODD is demanding, and taking time for yourself is crucial to maintaining your well-being. Respite care services offer short-term care for your child, allowing you to take a break, attend to personal matters, or rest and recharge. These services, often provided by qualified caregivers or specialized organizations, ensure your child is safe, allowing you to take necessary breaks without guilt. Understanding how to access these services through local community boards, social services, or specialized agencies can add an essential layer of support to your parenting strategy, ensuring you can replenish your energy and continue providing the best care for your child.

Building and maintaining a robust support network is not just about finding help; it's about creating a community that uplifts, understands, and walks with you as you navigate the challenges of raising a child with ODD. Whether through online platforms, local groups, informal friendships, or respite care, each element of this network plays a crucial role in supporting your parenting journey and your personal well-being.

8.4 BALANCING PARENTING AND PERSONAL LIFE

In the intricate dance of life, where parenting often takes center stage, it's vital to remember that maintaining a balanced perspective is critical. Establishing realistic expectations for both yourself and your child can significantly reduce the pressures associated with raising a child who has Oppositional Defiant Disorder (ODD). It's easy to fall into the trap of aiming for perfection—whether it's in your child's behavior, your parenting style, or in maintaining household harmony. However, it's essential to acknowledge that perfection is an unattainable and unrealistic goal. Instead, focus on celebrating progress and recognizing the effort. This change in mindset can alleviate frustration and disappointment for both you and your child, focusing the journey more on growth than reaching a perfect state.

Moreover, balancing life's demands often involves mastering prioritization and delegation skills. For parents, especially those managing the additional challenges of ODD, the day can feel like a series of tasks that must all be completed to perfection. By learning to prioritize these tasks based on urgency and importance, you can alleviate the feeling of being overwhelmed. Start by listing daily tasks and identify which are essential and can be postponed or skipped without significant consequences. Delegation plays a crucial role here. Engaging other family members in household responsibilities lightens your load and fosters a sense of teamwork and belonging. Whether assigning simple chores to your children or sharing responsibilities with a partner, effective delegation can lead to more manageable days.

Preserving personal interests and hobbies might seem like a luxury when faced with the relentless demands of parenting. However, engaging in activities you love is not an indulgence but a necessity. These activities provide a vital outlet for stress and allow you to maintain a sense of self separate from your parent role. Whether it's painting, hiking, reading, or any other activity that you're passionate about, make time for these pursuits. They are essential for your mental health and contribute to a well-rounded life, ensuring you remain energized and engaged in all facets of your life, including parenting.

For parents in a partnership, navigating the complexities of parenting a child with ODD can strain even the most vital relationships. Couple therapy can be valuable in these situations, offering a space to openly communicate each partner's feelings and challenges. This therapy can help strengthen the relationship by improving communication skills, resolving conflicts, and aligning parenting strategies. For single parents, personal therapy can be equally beneficial. It provides a supportive environment to discuss challenges and successes, helping to alleviate stress and foster personal growth. Therapy can be a profound tool for gaining insights and developing strategies supporting personal well-being and effective parenting.

Balancing the demands of parenting with personal and relational needs is not just about managing time; it's about cultivating a fulfilling life that nurtures all aspects of your being. By setting realistic expectations, prioritizing tasks, maintaining personal interests, and seeking therapeutic support, you can create a balanced life that enhances your ability to parent effectively and enjoy a rich, satisfying personal life. This approach benefits you and models healthy lifestyle habits for your child, demonstrating that taking care of oneself is both a priority and a necessity.

As we conclude this self-care and stress management chapter, we reflect on the essential strategies that fortify your resilience and enhance your capacity to nurture a positive family environment. From integrating mindfulness and physical wellness into your daily routine to building and maintaining a supportive community, each element contributes to your overall well-being and empowers you to meet parenting challenges with renewed strength and clarity. The next chapter will explore empowering strategies through understanding and action, guiding you to harness your knowledge and resources to advocate for your child and foster an environment of growth and learning.

CHAPTER 9
EMPOWERMENT THROUGH UNDERSTANDING AND ACTION

Empowerment begins when you realize that you are not alone in your journey and that there are actionable steps to enhance your child's life and your family's dynamics. This chapter unfolds the pivotal role of advocacy. This tool not only speaks but acts on behalf of your child with Oppositional Defiant Disorder (ODD). Here, we delve into understanding the various settings where advocacy is crucial, learning practical strategies to assert your child's needs, and navigating the legal landscapes that support these rights. By equipping yourself with these skills, you transform from a bystander to a proactive advocate, ensuring your child receives the support and understanding they deserve.

9.1 ADVOCATING FOR YOUR CHILD IN VARIOUS SETTINGS

Understand the Advocacy Landscape

Advocacy extends beyond the confines of home and touches every place your child interacts with others, including schools, medical facilities, and various social settings. Each arena offers unique challenges and opportunities for advocacy. In educational settings, advocating might mean working with teachers to implement or adjust Individual Education Plans (IEPs) that cater to your child's specific needs. During medical appointments, it involves communicating effectively with healthcare providers to ensure they understand your child's behavioral challenges and their impact on treatment options. Fostering a supportive environment might require educating friends, family, and community members about ODD in social settings.

Understanding where and when to advocate is crucial. It begins with recognizing situations where your child's unmet needs or rights might be overlooked. For instance, if your child is repeatedly punished in school for behaviors related to ODD without any supportive interventions in place, this is a clear signal that advocacy is needed to seek a better support system within the school.

Strategies for Effective Advocacy

Effective advocacy is rooted in clear, assertive communication. It's about expressing your child's needs in a way that is both respectful and firm, leaving no ambiguity about what is necessary for their success and well-being. Start by being well-prepared with all the required information about your child's condition, including diagnosis details, behaviors noted at home and in school, and any professional assessments or recommendations. This preparation makes your case stronger and your requests more compelling.

Negotiating for accommodations or support is another crucial aspect of effective advocacy. It involves asking for what your child needs and being open to discussing how these needs can be met within the existing framework. For example, suppose your child struggles with transitions during the school day. In that case, you might negotiate with the school to have a teacher or aide assist your child during these times.

Legal Rights and Resources

Understanding your child's legal rights is foundational in advocacy. Various laws protect the rights of children with disabilities, including those with behavioral disorders like ODD. Please familiarize yourself with laws such as the Individuals with Disabilities Education Act (IDEA) in the United States, which ensures students with a disability are provided with Free Appropriate Public Education (FAPE) tailored to their individual needs. Knowing these rights empowers you to advocate more effectively. It ensures that your child's educational and social environments are conducive to growth and development.

Additionally, many resources are available to support parents in this journey. Organizations such as the Child Mind Institute and the National Center for Learning Disabilities offer guidance and tools for advocacy, and connecting with local support groups can provide insights and collective knowledge that empower your advocacy efforts.

Role-Playing Scenarios

To bolster your confidence in advocacy, consider engaging in role-playing exercises. These scenarios can prepare you for real-life interactions and help you refine your communication and negotiation skills. For instance, practicing how you would discuss your child's needs with a teacher or doctor can alleviate some of the anxiety surrounding these conversations. Role-playing can be done with a partner, a friend, or even within a support group, where you can receive feedback and encouragement.

Interactive Element: Advocacy Role-Play Exercise

- Scenario: Preparing for an IEP meeting at school.
- Objective: To negotiate specific accommodations for your child.
- Process: Write down your main points. Practice presenting these points assertively. Have a partner respond as the teacher or school administrator might, and practice how you would counter their concerns or suggestions.
- Reflection: After the role-play, reflect on what strategies worked, what didn't, and how you can improve your advocacy in real situations.

By understanding the advocacy landscape, employing effective strategies, knowing your legal rights, and practicing your skills in safe environments, you are equipped to advocate for your child. This chapter aims to educate and empower you to take actionable steps that ensure your child is supported, understood, and valued in all aspects of life.

9.2 THE IMPORTANCE OF CONSISTENT PARENTING TECHNIQUES

Navigating the complexities of parenting a child with Oppositional Defiant Disorder (ODD) can often feel like trying to build a puzzle with moving pieces. Consistency in your parenting techniques provides a stable structure that helps you and your child understand and predict how to act and react in various situations. The benefits of such consistency are manifold, reducing confusion and providing a stable environment that can significantly alleviate the stress you and your child might experience. When expectations are clear and consistently applied, your child has fewer uncertainties about how their behaviors will be met, which can lead to a decrease in defiance and an increase in cooperative behavior.

Establishing and maintaining consistency, especially in a household with a child who tests boundaries, is no small task. It requires a clear understanding of the rules and expectations—not just for you but for everyone in your family. Consistency means that the rules are the same from one day to the next, and the consequences of actions are predictable. This doesn't mean rigidity; it's about having reliable guidelines that govern responses and consequences. For instance, if the rule is that no electronics are allowed during dinner, this should be a standard every evening, and all caregivers should enforce it. Consistency in enforcement helps your child internalize what is expected of them and understand the stability of these expectations, which can lead to better self-regulation over time.

One effective strategy for maintaining this consistency involves having clear, written rules. A visual reminder of the rules helps both children and adults remember them. Create a family rules chart that outlines what is expected and the consequences for failing to meet these expectations. Place this chart in a common area where it's easily visible, thus keeping everyone accountable. Review this chart regularly with your child, discussing each rule to ensure they understand the rule itself and its reasoning. This reinforces the rules and engages your child in the process, making them more likely to follow these guidelines.

However, despite the best plans, inconsistencies can and do occur. Handling these inconsistencies effectively is crucial in maintaining the efficacy of your parenting approach. It's essential to address these lapses when rules are overlooked or not followed. Discuss openly with your child why the inconsistency occurred, reaffirm the importance of the rule, and recommit to enforcing it consistently in the future. Find that a particular rule is consistently challenging to implement. It may be time to consider why this is happening. Is the rule too rigid? Is it not appropriate for your child's age or maturity? Reflecting on and adjusting your approach can be a sign of responsive and responsible parenting, not a failure to be consistent.

Family Meetings as a Tool

Regular family meetings can be excellent for discussing and reinforcing rules and techniques. These meetings provide a forum for the family to come together, discuss the rules, share feelings and concerns, and collectively find solutions to problems. During these meetings, please encourage your child to express their thoughts about the rules and any challenges they face. This helps them feel heard and valued and gives them a sense of participation and control over their environment, which can be particularly empowering for children with ODD.

During family meetings, make it a practice to review the family rules chart. Discuss each rule and its importance, and ask for input on what might need to be adjusted. These discussions can lead to a better understanding of what works and what doesn't, allowing you to tailor your strategies to better meet your child's and your family's needs. It's also a time to celebrate successes and address any discrepancies in rule enforcement. Doing this reinforces the importance of consistency and collective responsibility in maintaining a harmonious household.

Moreover, these meetings can be instrumental in teaching your child valuable life skills such as problem-solving, negotiation, and compromise. When children see that their opinions can influence family decisions and that problems can be discussed and resolved together, they learn important lessons about cooperation and communication. These skills are not only beneficial within the family but also help them navigate social relationships outside the home.

Regular family meetings, held in a spirit of openness and cooperation, can strengthen the bonds between family members and reinforce the structure and stability crucial in managing a household with a child with ODD. They serve as a reminder that while the journey might be challenging, it is one that you navigate together as a family, continually adapting and supporting each other along the way.

9.3 EDUCATING RELATIVES AND FRIENDS ABOUT ODD

When navigating the complexities of raising a child with Oppositional Defiant Disorder (ODD), the support and understanding of your extended family and friends become invaluable.

However, without a proper understanding of what ODD entails, well-intentioned comments or actions from relatives and friends can sometimes do more harm than good, leading to misunderstandings and additional stress for both you and your child. This is why educating those around you about ODD helps create a supportive environment and enhances your child's overall quality of interactions within their broader social circle.

Importance of Broad Understanding

ODD can often be misunderstood as just 'bad behavior' or poor parenting, which is far from the truth. It is a complex behavioral disorder that requires careful management and understanding. When relatives and friends comprehend ODD's challenges and nature, their approach towards your child can become more empathetic and supportive. This broader understanding can significantly reduce the stigma and isolation that many families dealing with ODD experience. It helps in normalizing the conversation about behavioral disorders, which can be particularly empowering for your child, showing them that they are not alone or 'different' in a negative sense. Moreover, when friends and family understand the reality of ODD, they are better equipped to offer help in meaningful ways, whether giving you a much-needed break or assisting in handling a difficult situation with your child.

Information Sharing Techniques

Sharing information about ODD can be approached delicately and thoughtfully. Start with simple explanations that encapsulate what ODD is and how it affects your child's behavior. For instance, ODD involves a pattern of angry, irritable mood, defiant behavior, and vindictiveness that goes beyond a typical child's occasional temper tantrums or rebellious phases. It's helpful to describe specific examples of ODD behaviors, making them more relatable and easier to understand.

Preparing a small, easy-to-read pamphlet or an email outlining key points about ODD can be a practical approach. Include bullet points on what ODD might look like, what triggers might exacerbate behaviors, and what strategies effectively manage these behaviors. This resource can be a quick reference for friends and family when needed. Additionally, recommending books, reputable websites, and articles that offer deeper insights into ODD can encourage them to learn more at their own pace. Websites such as the American Academy of Child & Adolescent Psychiatry or advocacy groups like the Child Mind Institute provide scientifically-backed information that can be trusted.

Setting Boundaries and Expectations

Clear communication about what behaviors or comments are not helpful or might be harmful is crucial in setting boundaries with relatives and friends. This might include asking them to avoid punitive measures, dismissive comments, or behavior contradicting your management strategies. For example, using positive reinforcement as a strategy would be counterproductive for a family member to employ harsh disciplinary measures for the same behaviors.

Setting these boundaries early and revisiting them as needed can prevent misunderstandings and ensure your child receives consistent messages from all the adults they interact with. It's also helpful to express what kind of support you appreciate. Whether respecting your rules when your child is at their house or offering to spend time with your child to give you a break, letting your family and friends know how they can help can benefit everyone involved.

Resource Distribution

Providing tangible resources can enhance understanding and support. Distribute pamphlets, books, or links to websites offering comprehensive ODD information. For a more interactive approach, consider organizing a casual meeting or a workshop where a professional can speak about ODD, and relatives and friends can ask questions. This can be an effective way to address various misconceptions and provide a platform for open discussion. Additionally, sharing documentaries or videos depicting real-life ODD scenarios can offer insightful perspectives and foster a more profound empathy and understanding among your relatives and friends.

Educating your extended network about ODD is about gaining their support and creating an informed community that upholds the dignity and respect every child deserves. This informed network can become a powerful ally in navigating the challenges of ODD, ensuring your child grows up in an environment where they are understood and supported, not just at home but in every circle they are part of.

9.4 THE FUTURE OF ODD: TRENDS AND RESEARCH

As we continue to advance our understanding of Oppositional Defiant Disorder (ODD), staying abreast of the latest research findings not only enhances our knowledge but also empowers us as parents to advocate for and apply the most effective interventions. Recent research has illuminated the complex nature of ODD, revealing that its development is influenced by a blend of genetic, environmental, and psychological factors. This nuanced understanding helps refine treatment approaches that are more personalized and effective. For instance, research has identified specific genetic markers that may increase susceptibility to ODD, suggesting that future treatments could include targeted therapies designed to address these genetic influences.

Additionally, the evolving landscape of behavioral therapy offers promising new directions for managing ODD. One emerging trend is integrating technology with traditional therapy methods, such as virtual reality (VR) environments, to simulate real-world scenarios where children can practice coping strategies in a controlled, safe setting. This method has shown potential in helping children with ODD develop better impulse control and frustration tolerance. Another innovative approach is using biofeedback techniques, where children learn to control certain body functions, such as heart rate, to improve their emotional and physiological responses to stress. These cutting-edge therapies highlight the dynamic nature of the field and its move towards more interactive and engaging treatment modalities.

The impact of societal changes on mental health perceptions also plays a critical role in shaping the experience of families dealing with ODD. As awareness and understanding of mental health issues continue to grow, stigma surrounding disorders like ODD decreases, leading to more open discussions and greater acceptance. This cultural shift is crucial as it influences everything from policy-making to everyday interactions in schools and communities, creating more inclusive and supportive environments for individuals with behavioral disorders. Moreover, societal acceptance encourages more families to seek help early, improving the chances of successful management and integration of children with ODD into various social settings.

Encouraging parental involvement in research is vital for advancing our understanding of ODD. Parents' unique insights and experiences can provide invaluable data that enhance the scientific community's knowledge of the disorder. By participating in research studies, parents can contribute to developing more effective strategies and treatments that will benefit their children and countless others across the globe. Researchers often seek participants for studies that explore new therapies, the effectiveness of current approaches, or the genetic and environmental factors contributing to ODD. Engaging in this research can be incredibly rewarding, as it offers a sense of contributing to meaningful advancements in the field.

Furthermore, developing parent-focused interventions is an area of growing interest, recognizing parents' crucial role in managing ODD. These programs are designed to support parents in adopting techniques that promote positive behaviors, reduce conflicts, and enhance family dynamics. By empowering parents with knowledge and practical skills, these interventions improve the child's behavior and enhance the parents' confidence and effectiveness in handling the challenges posed by ODD.

As we look to the future, it is clear that our understanding and management of Oppositional Defiant Disorder will continue to evolve. The integration of new research findings, the development of innovative therapeutic approaches, and the ongoing changes in societal attitudes towards mental health are all paving the way for more effective and compassionate management of ODD. For parents navigating this path, staying informed about these developments is crucial. It enables them to provide the best possible support for their children, ensuring they have the tools and understanding necessary to lead fulfilling lives despite the challenges of ODD.

9.5 WHEN TO UPDATE YOUR STRATEGIES: SIGNS OF EVOLVING NEEDS

As your child grows and develops, so too should the strategies you employ to manage and support their behavior, especially when navigating the complexities of Oppositional Defiant Disorder (ODD). Recognizing when and how to update your management strategies is crucial for effectively meeting your child's changing needs. It's a dynamic process reflective of the ever-evolving nature of both development and the disorder itself. This adaptability ensures that interventions remain effective and resonate with your child as they mature, fostering better outcomes and sustained progress.

Recognize Signs of Change

The first step in this adaptive process is to develop a keen sense of observation regarding changes in your child's behavior and the effectiveness of current strategies. Signs that indicate a need for adjustment in your approach include a noticeable increase in the frequency or intensity of behavioral issues or a need for improvement despite consistent application of current strategies. For instance, techniques that worked well in managing tantrums in a younger child might become less effective as the child approaches adolescence, necessitating new approaches that respect their growing desire for autonomy and self-regulation.

Another sign to watch for is your child's response to discipline and rewards. What motivated them a year ago may no longer hold the same appeal or influence. This shift can often be subtle, so staying attuned to their reactions and feedback can provide valuable clues that a change is needed. As children develop, they encounter new environments and challenges, such as transitioning from elementary to middle school or dealing with more complex social dynamics. These changes can introduce new triggers or stressors that might require adjustments to your existing management plan.

Adaptation Strategies

Once you've identified the need for a strategy update, the next step is determining how best to adapt your approach to fit your child's current needs. This might involve tweaking existing strategies to make them more age-appropriate or introducing new techniques catering to advanced developmental stages. For instance, while a simple timeout might have been a practical consequence for a younger child, an older child might benefit more from logical consequences that involve a discussion about the impact of their actions on others, fostering empathy and self-awareness.

In some cases, mainly where there are significant concerns or unsure how to proceed, seeking professional advice can be invaluable. Therapists or counselors specializing in ODD can offer guidance tailored to your child's situation, suggesting interventions based on the latest research and best practices. They can also help you to set realistic goals and expectations, providing support and reassurance as you navigate any necessary changes.

Regular Review and Adjustment

Regularly reviewing your management strategies is essential for ensuring they remain effective. This doesn't mean waiting for problems to arise but proactively assessing the situation at regular intervals—say, every few months—to determine what's working and what isn't. During these reviews, consider all aspects of your current strategies, from the triggers and behaviors they address to the ease with which they can be consistently applied. It's also important to consider the feedback from everyone involved, including teachers, therapists, and family members, and most importantly, from your child themselves.

Adjustments should be carefully considered, weighing the potential benefits against the stability of maintaining familiar routines. It's a delicate balance, requiring flexibility and patience. As you make these adjustments, keep detailed records of changes and responses, as this information can be precious for understanding what works best for your child and why.

Involving the Child in Updates

As children with ODD grow, they develop a greater capacity for self-reflection and understanding their own needs and triggers. Involving them in discussions about management strategies respects their growing autonomy and enhances the effectiveness of any adjustments you make. When children feel that their input is valued, they are more likely to be cooperative and actively manage their behavior.

Encourage your child to share their feelings about the strategies you're using: What do they find helpful? What do they dislike? What ideas do they have for making things work better? This can be done during family meetings or one-on-one discussions, providing a safe space for them to express themselves openly and honestly. Actively involving your child in this way not only promotes a more profound understanding on your part but also empowers them, boosting their confidence and their commitment to working towards positive change.

9.6 HARNESSING TECHNOLOGY: APPS AND TOOLS FOR MANAGING ODD

In the digital age, technology offers unique tools to significantly enhance the strategies used to manage Oppositional Defiant Disorder (ODD). The options are vast and varied, from apps that track behavior and mood to interactive games that teach emotional regulation. Introducing these tools into your management plan provides real-time data and consistent tracking. It engages your child in a medium they are likely familiar with and enjoy. This technology integration can make managing ODD more dynamic and practical, offering you and your child innovative ways to understand and control the disorder.

When exploring the array of apps available, you'll find that behavior-tracking apps can be particularly beneficial. These apps allow you to record instances of specific behaviors, track improvements or escalations and often offer the ability to share this data directly with therapists or educators involved in your child's care. This ongoing record can be invaluable in understanding patterns or triggers of behaviors, making it easier to tailor interventions more effectively. Mood diaries are another helpful tool, allowing your child to express and track their emotions. This self-reflection can be a decisive step in emotional regulation, helping them recognize their feelings and the circumstances that might influence their mood.

Using these apps and tools provides several benefits. The consistency of data collected through apps allows for a clear, unbiased look at progress and challenges, which can sometimes be obscured by the emotional stress of daily incidents. Immediate feedback from these apps can reinforce positive behavior changes for your child; for instance, seeing a visual representation of their progress in a behavior-tracking app can be a strong motivator. Additionally, sharing information with professionals helps ensure everyone involved in your child's care is on the same page, making coordinated efforts more streamlined and effective.

However, choosing the right apps and tools is crucial. When selecting an app, consider the privacy of the data it collects to protect your child's information. User-friendliness is another critical factor; the app should be easy for you and your child to use if it becomes a regular routine. Lastly, look for apps that are based on reputable, evidence-based practices. Check reviews or seek recommendations from professionals to find apps that are both engaging and therapeutically valid.

Integrating technology with traditional approaches to managing ODD should be done thoughtfully. While apps can support and enhance traditional methods, they should not replace them. Instead, use technology as a complementary tool. For instance, while a behavior-tracking app can give you insights into behavior patterns, direct interactions and discussions about those behaviors are crucial for making meaningful changes. Similarly, while an app might teach skills for emotional regulation, practicing these skills in real-life situations is essential for them to be truly effective.

By thoughtfully integrating technology into your management strategy, you harness a powerful ally in the quest to manage ODD effectively. Apps and tools offer a modern approach to tracking, understanding, and teaching, providing children and parents with innovative resources that can significantly improve their handling of the challenges of ODD.

In wrapping up this chapter on empowerment through understanding and action, we've explored how technology can play a pivotal role in managing ODD, complementing traditional methods with digital innovations that offer new insights and ways to engage. As we transition into the next chapter, we will continue to explore additional strategies and insights that can further enhance your ability to support and advocate for your child, ensuring they have the resources and understanding they need to thrive. Chapter 10 Real-Life Success Stories and Case Studies

CHAPTER 10
REAL-LIFE SUCCESS STORIES AND CASE STUDIES

Imagine finding a roadmap that guides you through the often tangled and obscure paths of parenting a child with Oppositional Defiant Disorder (ODD). This chapter delves into the heartwarming and inspiring journeys of families like yours, who have navigated the turbulent waters of severe defiance and emerged stronger. These narratives are not just stories but beacons of hope and practical guides illuminating the path to better family dynamics.

10.1 OVERCOMING SEVERE DEFIANCE: A FAMILY'S JOURNEY

Let's explore the compelling journey of the Thompson family, whose life was once dictated by the severe defiant behaviors of their son, Alex. At eight, Alex's interactions were often marked by intense confrontations, verbal outbursts, and a refusal to comply with most forms of authority, from parental commands to classroom rules. The Thompsons felt isolated, often misunderstood by friends and relatives who saw Alex's behaviors as disciplinary failures on the part of his parents.

Determined to seek change, the Thompsons embarked on a comprehensive strategy involving a multi-faceted approach to managing Alex's defiance. They turned to behavioral techniques that included consistent use of positive reinforcement for compliant and positive behaviors and precise, predictable consequences for defiance. Each strategy was applied consistently, with both parents united in their approach, ensuring Alex received the same messages and expectations from both. This consistency was crucial; it provided Alex with the clear boundaries he needed and, significantly, the security of knowing what to expect from his interactions with his parents.

Patience played a pivotal role in the Thompsons' strategy. Change did not occur overnight, nor was the journey linear. There were setbacks and days when old behaviors resurfaced, testing their resolve and patience. However, through the persistent application of their strategies and by choosing to celebrate small victories, the Thompsons gradually saw a decrease in Alex's defiant behaviors. The key was their commitment to the long-term goal rather than focusing on immediate results.

Support systems were integral to their success. The family engaged in regular therapy, involving not just Alex but all family members. This family therapy became a cornerstone of their approach, helping to address underlying emotional triggers for Alex's behaviors and, equally, helping family members understand their responses and how these could be adapted to better support Alex. Support groups also played a role, providing the Thompsons access to other families navigating similar challenges. These groups were invaluable, offering practical advice and emotional support that helped reduce their sense of isolation.

Several key lessons emerge from the Thompsons' journey that can enlighten and inspire other parents. Firstly, understanding the child's underlying emotional needs is crucial. Alex's defiance was not merely willful behavior but a manifestation of more profound emotional struggles that needed addressing. Secondly, the role of a united parental front cannot be overstated. Consistency in applying strategies provides the child with a sense of security and predictability. Lastly, the value of external support systems—in the form of therapy and support groups—provides guidance and crucial emotional support for the family.

This narrative underscores that while the path through ODD is undoubtedly challenging, positive change is a possible and reachable goal with the right strategies, patience, and support. The journey of the Thompson family is a testament to the power of resilience and informed, compassionate parenting. As we move forward in this chapter, let these stories remind you that you are not alone in this journey and that improvement and harmony are within your reach with the right approach.

10.2 INNOVATIVE SCHOOL APPROACHES THAT WORKED

In an era where educational flexibility is increasingly pivotal, one school's novel approach to managing a student with Oppositional Defiant Disorder (ODD) stands out as a beacon of innovation and empathy. At the heart of this strategy was introducing a customized behavioral plan meticulously tailored to meet the specific needs of a young student named Emily. The school recognized that traditional disciplinary tactics were ineffective and often exacerbated Emily's challenges, leading to frequent conflicts and academic struggles. As a proactive measure, the school implemented a plan that included specialized training for teachers on

ODD, peer mentors, and structured, predictable routines explicitly designed for Emily.

The collaboration between Emily's parents and the school was instrumental in crafting and refining this behavioral plan. Regular meetings were scheduled to ensure all parties could provide input and discuss progress. These sessions served as a platform for transparent communication, allowing for real-time adjustments to strategies and interventions based on Emily's evolving needs. This ongoing dialogue ensured that the strategies implemented at school were consistent with those used at home, providing Emily with a seamless support system that spanned both environments. The parents also facilitated workshops for teachers and staff, sharing insights and strategies that had been effective at home, which helped foster a deeper understanding and a more supportive school environment.

The outcomes of this tailored approach were transformative for Emily. She began to thrive academically, showing marked improvements in areas where she had previously struggled. Perhaps even more significantly, her social interactions had a noticeable enhancement. The peer mentor program, which paired Emily with older, empathetic students trained to understand and navigate the challenges associated with ODD, proved particularly beneficial. These mentors supported Emily during transitions between classes, lunchtime, and other social activities, which had been significant stress points for her. This support alleviated Emily's anxiety and fostered meaningful friendships that enhanced her social skills and self-esteem.

For parents looking to advocate for similar innovative approaches in their child's school, the key lies in proactive and informed advocacy. Begin by gathering comprehensive information about your child's specific needs and the interventions that have proven effective. Approach the school administration collaboratively, presenting your findings and suggesting a meeting to discuss potential strategies. Prepare to offer concrete examples of successful approaches, like the customized behavioral plan and peer mentoring system used in Emily's case, and explain how these can be adapted to fit your child's school environment. It's also beneficial to connect with other parents or local advocacy groups to strengthen your proposal, showing a united front that can help persuade school officials to consider and implement these innovative strategies.

This example underscores the profound impact that tailored educational strategies and strong collaboration between parents and schools can have on a child with ODD. Schools can play a pivotal role in shaping a more positive and productive educational experience for students with behavioral challenges by focusing on individual needs and fostering an environment of support and understanding.

10.3 THERAPY BREAKTHROUGHS: CHILDREN'S TESTIMONIALS

Therapy often serves as a transformative tool for children with Oppositional Defiant Disorder, providing them with techniques and insights that profoundly impact their everyday lives. To truly understand the value of these therapeutic interventions, we turn to the children's voices, whose firsthand experiences shed light on the practical benefits and personal growth they've achieved through therapy.

One vivid example comes from Lucas, a twelve-year-old who struggled significantly with anger management and interpersonal relationships before engaging in Cognitive Behavioral Therapy (CBT). Lucas shares, "Before therapy, everything felt like a battle, whether with my parents or friends. I didn't know how to handle my anger; I would explode. But in therapy, I learned about 'thinking traps.' These are ways your thoughts can trick you into reacting without considering other options. Identifying these traps helped me pause and think before reacting." Lucas's experience highlights a central component of CBT—cognitive restructuring, which helps children like him recognize and modify unhelpful thought patterns. This intervention didn't just help Lucas manage his anger; it equipped him with tools to improve his relationships by reacting more thoughtfully to frustrations.

Emma, a ten-year-old with ODD, learned that mindfulness exercises were particularly transformative. This technique was introduced to her during therapy; these practices helped her develop a greater awareness of her emotions and their impact on her behavior. Emma describes her experience: "My therapist taught me to notice what I feel in my body when I start to get mad—like a tight stomach or clenched fists. We practiced breathing exercises, and I learned to take deep breaths to calm down. It's like hitting a pause button on my feelings." This technique of mindfulness not only provided Emma with immediate ways to cope with rising emotions and fostered a skill set that enhanced her self-regulation. The daily application of these mindfulness strategies significantly reduced her reactive behaviors. It improved her ability to engage calmly in situations that previously would have triggered an outburst.

Beyond managing symptoms, therapy also offered these children a newfound understanding of their own emotions and behaviors, which is critical in reducing the stigma they often feel about their disorder. Jack, an eleven-year-old who participated in group therapy sessions, expressed how these interactions changed his perspective: "Meeting other kids like me was really cool. I used to feel weird or bad because it was hard not to get upset. However, in group therapy, I learned that many of us have similar struggles. We shared tips, and it made me feel less alone. It also made me realize that I can control my reactions." Group therapy provided Jack with peer support and normalized his experiences, significantly reducing his feelings of isolation and self-judgment.

These testimonials underscore the profound impact that therapy can have on a child's ability to navigate the complexities of ODD. Whether through cognitive-behavioral techniques that reshape thinking patterns or mindfulness exercises that enhance emotional awareness and control, therapy arms these young individuals with the tools necessary for personal growth and improved daily functioning. Moreover, the therapeutic environment offers a supportive space where children can explore their feelings and develop healthier coping mechanisms, fostering resilience and a more optimistic outlook.

As we delve into these personal stories, it becomes evident that therapy is more than a treatment; it is a journey toward self-discovery and empowerment. Each session builds upon the next, gradually unveiling a path forward for the children and their families. These narratives of challenge, learning, and triumph are a testament to the transformative power of therapeutic intervention in the lives of children with ODD.

10.4 PARENTS' STRATEGIES THAT TURNED BEHAVIOR AROUND

In the realm of parenting a child with Oppositional Defiant Disorder (ODD), a tapestry of strategies unfolds, each thread representing a unique approach woven by individual families to guide their children toward more adaptive behaviors. This strategy collection does not come from textbooks but from the living rooms, dinner tables, and bedtime routines of families who have walked this path before you. These are not just strategies; they are testaments to the resilience and creativity of parents committed to turning challenges into triumphs.

One effective strategy employed by the Martins involved structured choice-making. Faced with daily battles over tasks as simple as getting dressed or choosing breakfast, they decided to empower their son, Theo, by letting him make choices within defined limits. For instance, rather than instructing Theo to get ready for school, they offered him two outfit options and asked which one he would prefer to wear. This simple shift in approach reduced morning conflicts significantly. Implementing this required the parents to plan, ensuring appropriate choices were prepared. They faced challenges initially as Theo tested the limits of these choices. Still, through consistent application and clear boundaries, the strategy proved effective. The Martins found that this approach minimized conflict and enhanced Theo's sense of autonomy and decision-making skills.

Another family, the Nguyens, turned to a visual behavior chart to manage their daughter Ada's outbursts. Each day, Ada could earn stickers for positive behaviors and lose them for negative behaviors, with rewards aligned with her interests, like extra reading time or a family game night for accumulating a certain number of stickers. The visual nature of this system helped Ada see the immediate consequences of her actions, providing clear motivation for behavior change. The implementation phase was met with resistance, as Ada initially saw the system as another set of rules. However, her parents patiently guided her through the process, gradually helping her understand the benefits. This method improved Ada's behavior and taught her valuable lessons about consequences and rewards.

In a different approach, the Jackson family focused on de-escalation techniques to manage their son Eli's aggressive responses. They introduced a 'cool down' corner in their home, equipped with calming tools like stress balls, coloring books, and soft music. Whenever Eli felt overwhelmed or began to show signs of aggression, he was encouraged to go to his cool-down corner. This strategy required the parents to model the behavior using the corner when they felt stressed, demonstrating its effectiveness as a coping mechanism. Initially, Eli was reluctant to use the corner, viewing it as a punishment. Over time, however, he began to appreciate its value as a personal space to regain control over his emotions, significantly reducing the frequency and intensity of his outbursts.

These diverse strategies illustrate the importance of tailoring approaches to fit each child and family's unique needs and circumstances. Whether it's offering structured choices to foster independence, using visual aids to clarify behavioral expectations, or establishing safe spaces for emotional regulation, the underlying principles of consistency, patience, and understanding remain central. Each family's journey highlights the iterative process of finding what works best, making adjustments as needed, and the critical role of parental commitment in fostering lasting change.

As this chapter concludes, remember that each strategy presented here offers a glimpse into the possibilities of transformation. They are not just methods but are reflections of hope, perseverance, and the heartfelt dedication of families like yours. As we transition from these narratives of personal victory, let us carry forward the lessons learned, applying them with the same resolve and heart as those who shared their stories.

CONCLUSION

As we conclude our journey together through "Oppositional Defiant Disorder Simplified," I hope you've found a friend in these pages. This guide has walked you through understanding the foundations of ODD and embracing practical, effective strategies for communication, behavior management, and nurturing positive family dynamics. From exploring holistic and alternative approaches, delving into therapeutic interventions, and emphasizing the crucial role of parental self-care, each chapter was crafted to equip you with knowledge and tools to transform challenges into opportunities for growth.

The transformative power of knowledge and action cannot be overstated. By understanding the nuances of ODD and applying the strategies discussed, you can significantly enhance the quality of life for your child and your entire family. Remember, the keys to success in managing ODD include patience, perseverance, and maintaining a positive outlook, even when progress seems slow.

Here are the key takeaways we've covered:

- Understanding ODD and Its Foundations: Recognition of symptoms and early intervention can change the trajectory of ODD.
- Effective Communication Techniques: Tailored communication strategies are vital in reducing conflicts and enhancing understanding.
- Behavioral Management Techniques: Consistency and positive reinforcement play critical roles in shaping behavior.
- Building Positive Family Relationships: A united family approach strengthens the support system for ODD management.
- Holistic and Alternative Approaches: Broadening treatment strategies can enhance overall well-being.
- Therapeutic Interventions and Supports: Professional guidance is invaluable in navigating ODD.
- Parental Self-Care and Stress Management: Taking care of yourself is essential to being there fully for your child.
- Handling Everyday Challenges: Daily routines and prepared strategies reduce stress and improve outcomes.
- Empowerment Through Understanding and Action: Being informed and proactive empowers you to advocate effectively for your child.

Managing ODD is undeniably dynamic, requiring you to adapt and learn as your child grows. Stay abreast of the latest research and remain flexible, adjusting your strategies to meet your family's evolving needs.

Involving everyone—from siblings to extended family—enhances your child's support network and integrates ODD's management into everyday life. It's a collective effort that enriches the entire family.

I encourage you to reach out for support, join groups, and connect with other families who understand your challenges. Sharing your journey can be incredibly therapeutic and reduces the isolation often felt in dealing with behavioral disorders.

Lastly, let us part with a message of hope and encouragement. Despite the challenges, there is a path forward—a chance for improved dynamics, deeper understanding, and mutual respect. Embrace your journey with compassion and resilience; know you are not alone.

Please share your thoughts on this book and your experiences with me. Your feedback is invaluable, and your stories of progress and success inspire us in this community. Engage with us on social media or join local support groups to continue growing together.

Thank you for allowing me to be a part of your journey. Here's to a future where every challenge is met with courage, and every small victory is celebrated with joy.

With all my best, Charlene Collins

KEEPING THE GAME ALIVE

Now you have everything you need to support and inspire individuals with Oppositional Defiant Disorder (ODD), it's time to pass on your newfound knowledge and show other readers where they can find the same help.

Simply by leaving your honest opinion of this book on Amazon, you'll show other caregivers, parents, and educators where they can find the information they're looking for and pass on your passion for helping those with ODD.

I appreciate your help. Passing on our knowledge keeps the understanding and management of ODD alive, and you're helping us to do just that.

>>Scan the QR code to leave your review on Amazon.<<

REFERENCES

Oppositional defiant disorder (ODD) - Symptoms and causes https://www. mayoclinic.org/diseases-conditions/oppositional-defiant-disorder/symptoms-causes/syc-20375831#:

A Biopsychosocial Model of the Development of Chronic ... https://www.ncbi. nlm.nih.gov/pmc/articles/PMC2755613/

What Is Oppositional Defiant Disorder (ODD)? https://childmind.org/article/ what-is-odd-oppositional-defiant-disorder/

Dispelling 6 Common Myths About Oppositional Defiant ... https://www. goodtherapy.org/blog/dispelling-6-common-myths-about-oppositional-defi ant-disorder-0117197/

Children with Oppositional Defiant Disorder - Bright Futures https://www. brightfuturesny.com/post/oppositional-defiant-disorder#:

Active Listening | Communicating | Essentials - CDC https://www.cdc.gov/ parents/essentials/toddlersandpreschoolers/communication/activelistening. html#:

Emotional validation: A fundamental need in childhood and ... https://www. sinews.es/en/emotional-validation-a-fundamental-need-in-childhood-and-adolescence/

ODD in Children: A Parent's Behavior Management Guide https://www.addi tudemag.com/odd-in-children-adhd-management-strategies/

Positive Reinforcement vs. Bribery https://marybarbera.com/positive-reinforce ment-vs-bribery/

Parenting with Natural and Logical Consequences https://extension.okstate. edu/fact-sheets/print-publications/t/parenting-with-natural-and-logical-consequences-t-2390.pdf

How to Tailor Discipline to Your Child's Temperament https://www.verywell family.com/how-to-tailor-discipline-to-your-childs-temperament-1094786

12 family therapy activities to build trust and relationships https://kidsfunfam ily.com/12-family-therapy-activities-to-build-trust-and-relationships/

Exploring the Link Between Oppositional Defiant Disorder and ... https:// childpsychologycare.com/exploring-the-link-between-oppositional-defiant-disorder-and-family-dynamics

Oppositional defiant disorder (ODD) - Diagnosis and ... https://www.

mayoclinic.org/diseases-conditions/oppositional-defiant-disorder/diagnosis-treatment/drc-20375837

Parenting ODD Children and Teens: How to Make ... https://www.empowering parents.com/article/parenting-odd-children-and-teens-how-to-make-conse quences-work/

How Diet Can Heal Oppositional Defiant Disorder in Children https://www. livewithjoynow.com/how-diet-can-heal-oppositional-defiant-disorder/

Mental Health in Children: Yoga to the Rescue https://www.ideafit.com/mind-body-recovery/mental-health-in-children-yoga-to-the-rescue/

The Role of Art and Music Therapy Techniques in the ... https://www.sciencedi rect.com/science/article/pii/S1877042815018455/pdf?md5=b5cd d3f91c61a8e2772b2098941dde10&pid=1-s2.0-S1877042815018455-main.pdf

Sleep disturbance has the largest impact on children's ... https://www.fron tiersin.org/journals/pediatrics/articles/10.3389/fped.2022.1034057/full

Using Cognitive Behavior Therapy for Oppositional Defiant ... https://www. mghclaycenter.org/parenting-concerns/cbt-snapshot-using-cognitive-behav ior-therapy-for-oppositional-defiant-disorder-conduct-disorder/#:

The Pharmacological Management of Oppositional ... https://www.ncbi.nlm. nih.gov/pmc/articles/PMC4344947/

Individualized Education Programs (IEPs) (for Parents) https://kidshealth.org/ en/parents/iep.html

Support for Parents of Troubled Teens https://evolvetreatment.com/blog/ support-for-parents/

Self-care for parents https://www.unicef.org/parenting/mental-health/parent-self-care-tips

Mindfulness meditation: A research-proven way to reduce ... https://www.apa. org/topics/mindfulness/meditation

The 5 Benefits of Parent Counseling https://honoryouremotions.com/the-5-benefits-of-parent-counseling/

Parental Roles: How to Set Healthy Boundaries with Your Child https://www. empoweringparents.com/article/parental-roles-how-to-set-healthy-bound aries-with-your-child/

Creating a Stress-Free ADHD Morning Routine For Your Child https://www. theyarethefuture.co.uk/adhd-morning-routine/

5 Effective Strategies for Handling Your Child's Tantrums in ... https://www. oakridge.in/visakhapatnam/blogs/calming-the-storm-5-effective-strategies-for-handling-your-childs-tant